COMPREHENSIVE RESEARCH
AND STUDY GUIDE

# BLOOM'S

## MAJOR
## DRAMATISTS

*Eugène Ionesco*

EDITED AND WITH AN
INTRODUCTION BY HAROLD BLOOM

# CURRENTLY AVAILABLE

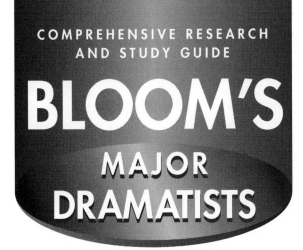

COMPREHENSIVE RESEARCH
AND STUDY GUIDE

# BLOOM'S
## MAJOR
## DRAMATISTS

# *Eugène Ionesco*

EDITED AND WITH AN INTRODUCTION
BY HAROLD BLOOM

CHELSEA HOUSE
PUBLISHERS
A Haights Cross Communications Company
Philadelphia

© 2003 by Chelsea House Publishers, a subsidiary of
Haights Cross Communications.

A Haights Cross Communications ✦ Company

Introduction © 2003 by Harold Bloom.

Printed and bound in the United States of America.

First Printing
1 3 5 7 9 8 6 4 2

Library of Congress Cataloging-in-Publication Data
Eugène Ionesco / edited and with an introduction by Harold Bloom.
        p. cm. —(Bloom's major dramatists)
Includes bibliographical references and index.
    ISBN 0-7910-7037-9
    1. Ionesco, Eugène—Criticism and interpretation. I. Bloom, Harold.
II. Series.
    PQ2617.06 Z6785 2002
    842'.914—dc21                                          2002012506


Chelsea House Publishers
1974 Sproul Road, Suite 400
Broomall, PA 19008-0914

www.chelseahouse.com


Contributing Editor: Robertson Erskine

Cover design by Terry Mallon

Layout by EJB Publishing Services

# CONTENTS

# USER'S GUIDE

This volume is designed to present biographical, critical, and bibliographical information on the author and the author's best-known or most important plays. Following Harold Bloom's editor's note and introduction is a concise biography of the author that discusses major life events and important literary accomplishments. A critical analysis of each play follows, tracing significant themes, patterns, and motifs in the work. An annotated list of characters supplies brief information on the main characters in each play.

A selection of critical extracts, derived from previously published material, follows each thematic analysis. In most cases, these extracts represent the best analysis available from a number of leading critics. Because these extracts are derived from previously published material, they will include the original notations and references when available. Each extract is cited, and readers are encouraged to use the original publications as they continue their research. A bibliography of the author's writings, a list of additional books and articles on the author and their work, and an index of themes and ideas conclude the volume.

As with any study guide, this volume is designed as a supplement to the works being discussed, and is in no way intended as a replacement for those works. The reader is advised to read the text prior to using this study guide, and to keep it accessible for quick reference.

# ABOUT THE EDITOR

Harold Bloom is Sterling Professor of the Humanities at Yale University and Henry W. and Albert A. Berg Professor of English at the New York University Graduate School. He is the author of over 20 books, and the editor of more than 30 anthologies of literary criticism.

Professor Bloom's works include *Shelley's Mythmaking* (1959), *The Visionary Company* (1961), *Blake's Apocalypse* (1963), *Yeats* (1970), *A Map of Misreading* (1975), *Kabbalah and Criticism* (1975), *Agon: Toward a Theory of Revisionism* (1982), *The American Religion* (1992), *The Western Canon* (1994), and *Omens of Millennium: The Gnosis of Angels, Dreams, and Resurrection* (1996). *The Anxiety of Influence* (1973) sets forth Professor Bloom's provocative theory of the literary relationships between the great writers and their predecessors. His most recent books include *Shakespeare: The Invention of the Human*, a 1998 National Book Award finalist, *How to Read and Why* (2000), and *Stories and Poems for Extremely Intelligent Children of All Ages* (2001).

Professor Bloom earned his Ph.D. from Yale University in 1955 and has served on the Yale faculty since then. He is a 1985 MacArthur Foundation Award recipient and served as the Charles Eliot Norton Professor of Poetry at Harvard University in 1987–88. In 1999 he was awarded the prestigious American Academy of Arts and Letters Gold Medal for Criticism. Professor Bloom is the editor of several other Chelsea House series in literary criticism, including BLOOM'S MAJOR SHORT STORY WRITERS, BLOOM'S MAJOR NOVELISTS, BLOOM'S MAJOR DRAMATISTS, BLOOM'S MODERN CRITICAL INTERPRETATIONS, BLOOM'S MODERN CRITICAL VIEWS, and BLOOM'S BIOCRITIQUES.

# EDITOR'S NOTE

My Introduction comments upon the sexual vampirism of the parody of teaching in *The Lesson,* and the fierce satire upon ideology in *The Rhinoceros.*

*The Bald Soprano*'s structure is analyzed by Richard Schechner, while the other critics center on questions of meaning and language.

There is less agreement on *The Lessons,* where sadism necessarily serves as a connective element in almost all commentary. I find particularly useful the insights of Nancy Lane, Deborah B. Gaensbauer, and Vicky Unruh on the Professor's violence.

*The Chairs* is examined from surprisingly different perspectives by six critics, including Albert Bermel on the play's vision of marriage, and Rosette C. Lamont on the allegory of aging.

*Rhinoceros,* still Ionesco's most popular work, tends to provoke simplistic analyses. Roy Arthur Swanson finds Orestes in Bérenger, while Matei Calinescu invokes the historical background of Romania's Fascist Iron Guard movement.

# Harold Bloom

*The Lesson*, in my experience, plays better than it reads. Properly directed and acted, it manifests a rising rhythm of sexual hysteria and violence profoundly disturbing to the audience. When the Maid tells us, after the murder, that the Professor has just dispatched his fortieth victim of the day, we are not immediately incredulous. Reading her assertion provokes more than skepticism: why not sixty, we might inquire? Ionesco's ferocious theater parable defies literalization, on a stage where philology is parodied as vampiric slaughter.

If *The Lesson* still works in the theater, after half a century, the credit goes less to politics, sexual or social, than to Ionesco's primordial sense of some of the foundations of drama. We watch a ritual sacrifice, though the ritual is a farce. Our Sexual Harassment Committees, so charming a feature of the current American academic scene, should attend compulsory performances of *The Lesson*, on a regular basis.

*Rhinoceros* also plays more strongly than even an acute reading could suggest. Anyone who saw Zero Mostel mug his metamorphosis into a rhinoceros is unlikely to forget it. At Yale, I have watched faculty members change into rhinoceroses steadily since the academic year 1969-70. To be sure, Political Correctness produces relatively amiable rhinoceroses, but a rhinoceros is a rhinoceros nevertheless. In honor of Ionesco, I have taken to calling one of our deans "Rataxes," the king of the rhinoceroses in the *Babar* books, which I used to read to my sons, when they were little.

Poor Bérenger is certainly a flawed hero: weak, confused, fearful, alcoholic. Yet he will not yield. No one can win the war against our rhinoceroses, and Bérenger doubtless will be gored, but he will die human.

# Eugène Ionesco

Eugène Ionesco was born on November 26th 1909 (the 13th according to the Orthodox calendar) in a small city outside of Bucharest, Romania. Many sources have records indicating 1912 as the year of his birth, suggesting that Ionesco may have mislead the public about his age later in life.

His father, Eugène Ionesco Sr. was a Romanian lawyer, and his mother, Thérèse Ipcar, was the daughter of a French engineer. Ionesco had a sister, Marilina, who was born on February 11th, 1911 and a younger brother, Mircea, who died of meningitis at the age of 18 months. Before Ionesco was a year old, his family moved to Paris where his father continued his education and eventually became a professor of Law in Paris.

His father returned to Bucharest in 1916 at the beginning of WWI, leaving his wife and the two young children to survive on their own in Paris, although with some support from Thérèse's parents. For several years, the family did not hear from the father, and they feared that he had died during the war. While in Paris, they lived in a dark apartment where Ionesco wrote a "heroic" play in two acts (32 pages in an exercise book) and a comic scenario. These texts were unfortunately lost.

Ionesco discovered that his father had not died in the war, but had obtained a position in the Bucharest police force and had remarried. His father was a strong supporter of the communists and of Nazi ideology, and his political alignment with these forces allowed him to convince authorities that Ionesco's mother had abandoned the children and that all custody should be granted to him.

In 1922 Ionesco and his sister returned to Bucharest to live with their father, during which time Ionesco completed a Bachelors degree. The living situation was uncomfortable for everyone involved, eventually leading to the further separation of the family. The relations with his father's family were strained, especially those with their stepmother who did not like them. The difficult living situation eventually drove Eugène's sister away, and in 1926, after a disagreement with his father, Ionesco would leave as well.

In 1928 he had his debut as a poet in *Bilete de papagal* (Parrot-Notes). A year later he began a degree in French at the University of Bucharest where he continued to write poetry—eventually publishing *Elegii pentru fiinte mici* (Elegies for Tiny Beings) in 1931. During this time he also wrote articles in *Vremea* (Time), *Azi* (Today), *Floarea de Foc* (Flower of Fire), *Viata Literara* (Literary Life), *România Literara* (Literary Romania), the weekly antifascist magazine *Critica*, *Axa* (the Axis), *Fapta* (the Fact), *Ideea*, *Româneasca* and *Zodiac*.

On July 8, 1936 Eugène Ionesco married Rodica Burileanu, and they spent their honeymoon in Constanza and Greece. This time of happiness was short lived; three months after the wedding, Ionesco's mother died of a stroke.

Ionesco spent the next few years writing and teaching French. His political opinions became more evident in his writing and by 1937 he was in charge of the critical section of the *Facla* review. He also published articles in *Universul Literar*, the cultural daily newspaper *Rampa* (the Slope), and *Parerile Libere* (Free Opinions). During the next few years, he traveled throughout France publishing various small pieces in Marseilles and Paris.

At the start of World War II, Ionesco returned to Romania where he worked as a French teacher at the secondary school of Sfântul Sava in Bucharest. He regretted his decision to return to Romania and spent the next few years trying to return to France. Finally in 1942, he successfully returned to France with his wife. Times were tough for the young couple as he worked as a translator spending a great deal of time translating and writing a preface for the novel "Urcan Batrânul" (Father Urcan) by Pavel Dan (1907-1937).

His daughter Marie-France was born on August 26, 1944. The next year the family decided to move to Paris where they established residence at the rue Claude-Terrace 38 where they would stay until 1960. While there, Ionesco worked as a proofreader for an administrative publisher, and between the years of 1945-1949 he spent most of his time translating the Romania surrealist poet Urmoz (1883-1923).

In 1948, the year that his father died, Ionesco began writing his first play. This would later evolve into *The Bald Prima Donna or The Bald Soprano*. Its first performance was at the Théâtre des Noctambules on May 11, 1950 under the direction of Nicolas Bataille. The play was not successful and was supported by only a select group of individuals who could understand the satirical theme in Ionesco's work.

Ionesco released a play every year for the next eight years: *The Lesson*, 1951; *The Chairs*, 1952; *Victims of Duty*, 1953; *Amédée or How to Get Rid of It*, 1954; *Jack, or The Submission*, 1955; *Improvisation or The Shepherd's Chameleon*, 1956; *The New Tenant* and *The Future is in Eggs*, 1957; *Rhinoceros (written)*, 1958; *Rhinoceros (performed)* and *The Killers*, 1959.

Ionesco's work came under great scrutiny in 1958. The debate between Ionesco and the English critic, Kenneth Tynan from *The Observer* became known as the "London Controversy." Tynan, an early enthusiastic supporter of Ionesco, decided after the premiere of *The Chairs* in 1957, that Ionesco's work was dangerous to the public claiming that Ionesco was trying to create a kind of cult. Ionesco defended his theatre and his vision of the theatre against the attacks.

1962 was a momentous year for Ionesco as four more of his plays premiered including *Exit the King, Notes and Counter-Notes, The Colonel's Photograph*, and *A Stroll in the Air*. In 1964 *Hunger and Thirst* met with a warm reception and was followed by *French Lessons for Americans (1966), The Gap (1966), Fragments of a Journal (1967), Present Past Past Present (1968), Découvertes (1969), The Killing Game (1970), Macbett (1972), The Hermit (1973), A Hell of a Mess (1973), The Man with the Luggage (1975), Antidotes (1977),* and *Journeys among the Dead (1980)*.

During this span of time, Ionesco received many awards and much recognition including the medal of Monaco and the Great National Theatre Prize in 1968.

In 1970, Ionesco was elected a member of the French Academy, taking over the seat of Jean Paulhan. That same year, he received the Great Austrian Prize of European literature. In addition, Ionesco was asked to make the opening speech at the Salzburg Festival in 1972.

On April 30, 1973 he received the Jerusalem Prize and in June the medal of the town of Vichy. In 1974 he received an honorary doctorate from the University of Warwick (UK) and another honorary doctorate in March 1975 from the University of Tel-Aviv. He received the Max Reinhardt-medal in August 1976 during the celebration of the 50th anniversary of the Salzburg Festival.

An extravagant ten-day tribute *La Décade Ionesco* took place from August 3-13 in 1978 where many of the leading Ionesco scholars of the world gathered in a chateau in Normandy. Paul Vernois and Marie-France Ionesco arranged the gathering, and Eugène and Rodica Ionesco attended the event for the last few days. Following the event many of the participants' contributions were collected and compiled into the book *Ionesco: Situation et perspectives.*

Ionesco continued to write and make appearances, but his health began to deteriorate, and in February 1984, he was hospitalized for two days suffering from diabetes. When his health returned, he continued to travel giving speeches and attending conferences. In 1985, Ionesco received the Monte-Carlo International Prize of Contemporary Art, and served as a member of the jury of the Venice Film Biennial.

On February 23, 1987, Théâtre de la Huchette celebrated the thirtieth anniversary of it's *The Bald Soprano* performance, in the presence of Eugène and Rodica Ionesco and many of the actors who, through the years, had taken turns participating in *The Bald Prima Donna* and *The Lesson.* Later that year he received the medal of the city of Paris.

Ionesco spent his last years traveling and speaking out against censorship and the inhumane treatment of people around the world.

Eugène Ionesco died on March 28, 1994 in his residence in Paris. He was buried in the Cemetery of Montparnasse.

# *The Bald Soprano*

*The Bald Soprano* is a statement about the absurd nature of human existence. Ionesco creates characters whose actions are mundane, repetitive, and meaningless. All of the events in the play revolve around two couples: the Smiths and the Martins. The only other characters are Mary, the Smiths' maid, and the Fire Chief.

The play begins with a clock, described as being a typical English clock, striking seventeen times as an English couple, the Smiths, are engaged in a meaningless conversation about their meal. The conversation is full of pointless clichés made by Mrs. Smith followed by Mr. Smith clicking his tongue in response to his wife's statements. Mr. Smith sits reading his newspaper, continuing to click his tongue in response to his wife's statements until the subject of Dr. Mackenzie-King is introduced. Mrs. Smith finds him to be a good doctor, but only because he does not prescribe medication unless he has tried it himself and also because he had an operation on his own healthy liver before he would operate on a patient's liver: Mr. Parker. Mr. Smith finds fault with her logic suggesting that he must not be a good doctor because Parker did not survive the operation. He does not think he is a bad doctor because Parker died; rather, that the Doctor lived and that a truly good doctor would have died as well. The conversation then turns to the death of their acquaintance, Bobby Watson.

While reading the paper, Mr. Smith mentions that Bobby Watson has died. This conversation quickly becomes confusing as everyone in the Watson family is named Bobby Watson. At this point in the play Mary, the Smith's maid enters, and informs the Smiths that their dinner guests, the Martins, are waiting down stairs. Mary is instructed to invite the Martins in as the Smiths prepare for their guests. This sequence of events is obviously a bit odd since the Smiths have just finished eating. Meanwhile, Mary shows the Martins in and takes them to the sitting room.

As Mary leaves the couple alone, they introduce themselves as though they have never met before. The stage instructions suggest that the actors use monotonous voices as they introduce themselves trying to discover why they look so familiar to one another. They discover with astonishment that they both are originally from Manchester, they both moved to London five weeks prior, they both took the same train, at the same time, and were in the same car when traveling to London. Furthermore, they discover that they sat across from one another and Mr. Martin helped Mrs. Martin with her luggage. This conversation continues as they discover that they live on the same street, in the same house, in the same room, and that they both have the same bedspread. They both marvel at this coincidence as they also uncover that they have the same daughter, named Alice, who has one red eye and one white eye. From all of this information the Martins deduce that they must be married. They embrace, kiss and vow never to lose one another again at which point Mary enters and informs the audience that the couple is mistaken and that actually they are not married, and that the Alice can not be their child because Mr. Donald Martin's daughter has a white right eye and a red left eye and Mrs. Martin (whom Mary addresses as Elizabeth) has a daughter with a white left eye and red right eye. After Mary makes this declaration, she proclaims that she is Sherlock Holmes and exits. At this point in the play the stage directions suggest that the clock should strike random hours.

The Smiths enter the sitting room and are outraged at the Martins for being so late. This is an odd situation since a few moments before the Smiths had just finished eating and during their meal they did not mention that they were expecting guests. They act as though there was nothing out of the ordinary until Mary informs them that the Martins had arrived. After Mr. Smiths' tirade about how rude it is to show up to dinner so late, the couples stare at each other for several minutes. They seem to be out of things to talk about although they have not had any conversation yet. They continue to stare at each other with an occasional "hmm" until Mrs. Martin breaks the silence. She describes how shocked and amazed she was to watch a man tie his shoelace on the train: everyone is amazed. Mrs. Smith, not wanting to be outdone in her own home, recounts an equally enticing story of a man on a train that she saw reading the newspaper: again the group is amazed at such odd behavior. As she finishes her tale the doorbell rings and Mrs. Smith goes to see who has arrived. She returns to inform the group that no one was at the door. The bell rings another two times with the same result.

The next section of the play is a pseudo philosophical debate about whether someone is always or never there when the doorbell rings. When the doorbell rings a fourth time Mrs. Smith refuses to go to the door, so Mr. Smith goes to the door and returns with the Fire Chief. He had been at the door for three-quarters of an hour, ringing the door and then hiding as a joke. He was patrolling the neighborhood looking for fires and inquired if they had any inside. Although the Fire Chief claims to be very busy searching for fires, he stays with the couples to tell stories. All the stories told by the Fire Chief begin like didactic fables suggesting that some lesson is being taught, but in the end none of them make sense.

The entrance of Mary, who wants to recite one of her poems, interrupts the storytelling time. The Smiths and Martins are amazed at Mary's insolence, but before she is chastised, she and the Fire Chief recognize each other as long lost sweethearts. She begins reciting her poem, which is really just a list of things that have caught on fire and the Smiths push her out the door. The Fire Chief is deeply moved by the poem. He begins making random connections between the poem and other events and eventually asks the couples if they have heard of the bald soprano. Upon uttering these words everyone becomes very embarrassed and the Fire Chief makes a hasty exit.

The final scene of the play entails the couples speaking to one another in cliché expressions like "One must always think of everything" and "Charity begins at home." These statements are uttered with increasing urgency and irritation even though there is no logical connection between them. Both couples use these phrases as though each one is a rebuttal of the others until they are screaming and grunting at one another. The final climax has the four of them screaming in unison "It's not that way, it's over here." The screaming ends abruptly and the lights go off. When the lights come on again the play has begun again this time with the Martins in the same opening scene instead of the Smiths.

LIST OF CHARACTERS IN

# *The Bald Soprano*

**Mr. Smith** is a middle-class Englishman married to a middle-class Englishwoman, Mrs. Smith. He is described in the stage settings as being an average Englishman wearing English slippers, smoking an English pipe, wearing English glasses and a small gray English mustache. The couple has three children: a young boy, and two daughters, Helen and Peggy. He does not really pay any attention to his wife, spending the first few pages of the play making a clicking noise when his wife addresses him. His only real comments to her are not exactly nurturing. He belittles her and intentionally says things that will upset her.

**Mrs. Smith** is, like her husband, middle-class and average in all respects. She is a doting wife. She is concerned about image and on one occasion warns her husband not to involve outsiders in family affairs even though the Martins have been present throughout the argument.

**Mr. Donald Martin** is a very polite Englishman who used to live in Manchester. He is married to Mrs. Martin but they do not appear to remember one another. He has a daughter, Alice, who has one red eye and one white eye.

**Mrs. Elizabeth Martin** is a middle class Englishwoman. She is married to Mr. Martin, but, like Mr. Martin, does not recognize him as her husband.

**Mary, the Maid** is the house servant for the Smiths. She has had an amorous relationship with the Fire Chief at some point in her past. She has some knowledge about all of the characters involved in the play, and she reveals to the audience that the Martins do not have a child together as they have suggested.

**The Fire Chief** patrols the city going door to door in search of fires. He is thought to be a great storyteller by both the Smiths and the Martins when in fact none of his stories make any sense. He is very much in love with Mary and is overjoyed with her poem that she recites for the couples.

# The Bald Soprano

## ALLAN LEWIS ON IONESCO'S STYLE

[Allan Lewis is a respected critic who has published a book about Ionesco. Other publication can be found in *Queen's Quarterly, Arts in Society, and Educational Theatre Journal*]

V *The Tragedy of Language*—"Philology leads to calamity."

The breakdown of existing logic implies the death knell of language and grammatical construction, the instrument of logical communication. Words are reduced to empty sounds and the platitude becomes a revelation of fresh insight. Inherited language patterns can only convey the sense of absurd relationships. Ionesco stresses banality, repetitions, incongruity, and exaggerations in the manner of surrealist painting. When he wrote *The Bald Soprano* he did not know how the play would end, but he did have in mind "the final breakdown of language and the resulting deterioration."

The two couples in *The Bald Soprano* explode in a rhythmic chant of nonsense syllables using the letters of the alphabet as a choral refrain. Language is worn and tired: "separated from life ... it is not so much necessary to reinvent it as to restore it." Entire scenes are constructed from alternating disconnected cliches, as in *The Bald Soprano*:

| | |
|---|---|
| MRS. SMITH: | One walks on his feet, but one beats with electricity or coal. |
| MRS. MARTIN: | He who sells an ox today, will have an egg tomorrow. |
| MRS. SMITH: | In real life, one must look out of the window. |
| MRS. MARTIN: | One can sit down on a chair, when the chair doesn't have any. |

Nuances of expression give way to a succession of platitudes. To the Professor in *The Lesson* all languages are identical. The word "cat" is all Roberta in *Jack* needs to express all concepts. The Old Man in *The Chairs* greets the Emperor with a humble obeisance and a dog's bark, "Your servant, your slave, your dog, arf, arf, your dog, Your Majesty."

Language is a weapon of a logical world to precipitate destruction. The Maid in *The Lesson* advises the Professor that "philology leads to calamity." Bérenger, facing the Killer, exhausts all the devices of language to reason with his enemy, who responds not with words but with variations of chuckles until Bérenger is left speechless and helpless, a victim of the failure of words. The human voices in *Rhinoceros* are stilled and only animal grunts are heard. Jean in *Hunger and Thirst* is reduced to listing the names of things in a ritual of recalled experiences. The Old Man in *The Chairs* shouts to the waiting but invisible world that he has discovered "absolute certainty," a parody of the scientific pronouncement of first causes and ultimate enlightenment. The speech is delivered by a deaf-mute who can only grunt.

If sound can induce tragedy, silence becomes an effective dramatic opposite and the interchange of the two is developed in planned orchestration. Ionesco, like Beckett, uses broken sentences, half phrases, monologues, and sudden pauses to intensity the surrounding climate of nothingness.

—Allan Lewis, "The Bald Soprano, The Lessons, The Chairs," *Ionesco.* New York: Twayne Publishers, Inc., 1972. 26-28.

## RICHARD SCHECHNER ON THE STRUCTURE OF *THE BALD SOPRANO*

[Richard Schechner is a Professor of Performance Studies at New York University. His publications include *Environmental Theater*, rev. ed. 1995, *The Future of Ritual* 1993, *Performance Theory* 1985, and *Between Theater and Anthropology* 1985]

In April, 1951, a few months after the world premiere of *The Bald Soprano* in Paris, and two years after the play was written, Ionesco began to talk about the structure of his play.

> *The Bald Soprano*, like *The Lesson*, among other things, attempts to make the mechanics of drama function in a vacuum. An experiment in abstract or non-representative drama. [...] The aim is to release dramatic tension without the help of any proper plot or any special subject. But it still leads, in the end, to the revelation of something monstrous: this is essential, moreover, for in the last resort drama is a revelation of monstrosity or of some monstrous formless state of being or of monstrous forms that we carry in ourselves. [...] The progression of purposeless passion, a rising crescendo that is all the more natural, dramatic, and exciting because it is not hampered by content, and by that I mean any apparent content or subject which conceals the genuine subject from us: the particular meaning of a dramatic plot hides its essential significance.[1]

Ionesco packs a lot of fundamental theory into these 175 words. He claims for his first two plays an architectural, structural pristinity; he says that drama is the revelation of that monstrous (and I am reminded here of Greek myth, and the myth-rites of many other peoples as well) rising suddenly and perplexingly from the depths, as a vast whale from the sea. He says that drama is best which is least plotted because the plot is a veil concealing the action of the play.

In 1970 these assertions may seem passé, but they are not. We must locate Ionesco's dramaturgy properly. He is a writer; he is talking about plays and not performances. He raises for us the questions of play structure, and questions put powerfully twenty years ago have not been resolved. Rather, performers have intervened and solved the questions for themselves (and, maybe, for the theater) by dismissing the writer and substituting the performer and the director. In considering Ionesco's claims we are, perhaps, delving into an archaic problem. But, I think, before we are through, we shall come to a fuller understanding of some current baffling situations. After all, we do not want to eliminate words from the theater, but find for them proper places. The writer is not the money-changer to be chased from the temple, nor even the hypocrite. He has simply been off somewhere, doing something else. And Ionesco was among the first to suggest through his theory and his practice how the writer might re-enter the work of the theater.

Ionesco wants to reveal the structure by sucking out the content. He is an architect and a musician. He is interested in what supports drama, where the connections are, and in what direction the stresses run. The process of writing led him from parody to originality, a very difficult circle to close.

> In my first play, *The Bald Soprano*, which started off as an attempt to parody the theatre, and hence a certain kind of human behavior, it was by plunging into banality, by draining the sense from the hollowest clichés of everyday language that I tried to render the strangeness and the farcical, the prosaic and the poetic, the realistic and the fantastic, the strange and the ordinary, perhaps these are the contradictory principles (there is no theatre without conflict) that may serve as a basis for a new dramatic structure. In this way perhaps the unnatural can by its very violence appear natural, and the too natural will avoid the naturalistic.[2]

Stripping away, as a technique, eliminates the accustomed order of things, the causative world, and reveals rhythms. These may be thoracic-like breathing and heartbeat—or "natural"-like sunrise and sunset; or even metaphysical and "logical" as when Mrs. Smith concludes that "experience teaches us that when one hears the doorbell ring it is because there is never anyone there." Here the structure of logical thought is laid out—namely, that one reasons from particular instances in accord with certain rules of induction and deduction. This structure is put up against the structure of theater—namely, that one can arrange whatever business one wishes.

Rhythms are automatic and often unconscious. They are patterns that are not necessarily causative. Night follows day but night does not cause day. To strip away the causative necessities that make a plot is to leave theater naked and to liberate the energies of rhythms. It is making theater approach music, that first art of rhythm-making and playing. These rhythms are alive in *Soprano*, but not the people, who are empty, mechanical, and dying. The drama's language is alive; it has its own logic, it reproduces itself (the play's climax), it creates people (Bobby Watsons), and situations (the courtship of the Martins). *Soprano* turns classic comedy on its head, and in doing so earns itself a place within the comic tradition. For that tradition is nothing other than finding new solutions to the oldest problem: how to beat death. Comedy does this by uncovering again and again life in the least likely places. In *Soprano* language is life. The obstacles to life are the Smiths and the Martins. As in the science-fiction film *The Invasion of the Body Snatchers*, a new life-force enters people, hollows them out, and takes over their shells. Inside the dead and dying people a new life-force stirs. It is not an evolution or a moral development. It is wholly new and alien.

*Soprano* opens with seventeen clangs of the clock—and Mrs. Smith says, "There it's nine o'clock." Her talking is automatic, as if whatever is speaking is not yet used to English. "We've drunk the soup and eaten the fish and chips," etc. Something is talking through Mrs. Smith, making its report, struggling with English grammar and vocabulary. (No wonder Ionesco punched through to the bottom of the opportunity of *Soprano* while studying English in the *Assimil* primer.) Mrs. Smith talks English, but her language is no longer her own, nor is it that of the alien being inside her. That being, language itself, is *learning English* just as Hal does in Kubrick's *2001*. It is the instrument closest at hand. What is the difference between "language" and "English"? English is one of the limitless forms language may take as its expression. Mrs. Smith is not aware that she is the host for an alien being. Why should she be—are you aware of the millions of bacteria in your gut? As she dies to her old life she becomes the means of the new life.

She reports how she feels. She looks at herself and her family as if they were at a far distance from her. She is not involved emotionally. In fact, each time she says "we" she could more correctly say "they." Of course, from one perspective this is a protest against the "dehumanization" of man; a typical theme of the forties and fifties. But I think we are ready for a new interpretation. Mrs. Smith is not using language. It is using her. She is "they" because language is "I." The language needs people because it is not able to live on its own, purely; people are its means of being, its host. But we ought not to prematurely or prejudicially abhor such a language. And surely we must not underestimate its power or deny to it *a priori* compassionate feelings. Some parasites are intelligent and cunning; and some the agents of high cultures. We have no reason to be contemptuous of these life-forms; such contempt is a function of ethnocentrism. "While writing this play," Ionesco says, "I felt genuinely uneasy, sick and dizzy. [...] When I had finished I was nevertheless very proud of it. I imagined I had written something like the tragedy of language."

The triumph of language is more like it. But Ionesco's malaise is understandable. He is writing of possession in its pure and absolute sense; writing from within the experience of being possessed. When Ionesco finished his play it appeared a tragedy because the author was unable to fly away from his humanity— he is no traitor to his species. But he is a traitor to an aspect of his culture—that part which values individualism above everything else. *Soprano* is triumphant, comic, buoyant, and proud if you do not value individualism. The author is dizzy because his whole career indicates a deep problem concerning individualism, about which he has the most ambivalent feelings.

Looking behind the drama at some of its social implications, some twenty years after its premiere, we recognize that language is the most salient stirring of a wholly vivified environment—a world of teeming life where not only words but gestures, clocks, doorbells, servants—things which we expect to be dehumanized, manageable, "in their places"—spring alive with shocking energy. The Smith and the Martins are dying; the Fire Chief is the messenger of a new culture (this needs looking at later); and Marie is a liberated woman—the maid who won't do what she's told, the Fire Chief's first lover, Sherlock Holmes.

Customarily we think of culture as the secretion of human

living and experience. To use a visual metaphor, human beings are the core and culture the meat of the apple. The relationship between the biological and the sociological species is as between core and meat. But *Soprano* reverses that. At the core is the cultural, and around that, serving it, are the people. What we experience in this drama is a world in which culture (language, things) is alive and the people are secretions and by-products. The Martins don't even know they are married until they discover so through deductive logic; and even then they are wrong (so Marie tells us). The Bobby Watsons proliferate as they are talked of because they are the children of language, not of human parents. The clock strikes as many times as it wants to. Sometimes when the doorbell rings there is someone there, and sometimes not. Even the stage directions have a rhetoric which identifies them with the rest of the drama, not with the author.

Words do not identify the Bobby Watsons. They live only as they can be talked about. They are the creations and the toys of a language just starting to explore its own possibilities. As Vannier says, "language has been promoted to the dignity of a theatrical object."[3] Words are no longer the vehicles of thoughts or feelings; they are themselves actions—the initiators of dramatic events. Conceivably, if we could *see* the Watsons we could tell old from young, male from female, living from dead.[4] But the Watsons do not exist as people offstage (anymore than the invisible people of *The Chairs* are "real"); the Watsons are what they are—part of a conversation. Language makes the Watsons, and language can multiply, confuse, kill, birth, or do what it wills with them. The Smiths cannot interfere with this wordplay because ultimately the Smiths are like the Watsons. As Mrs. Martin reminds Mr. Martin, "This morning when you looked at yourself in the mirror you didn't see yourself." And he nicely answers, "That's because I wasn't there yet."

In *Soprano* there is little conflict between the drama's protagonist—language—and the human beings. Even the mad dance finale is a dance of triumph, a celebration of language's liberation from people. Perhaps, as Doubrovsky believes, this is an indication of despair, a revelation of monstrosity.

Instead of using language to think, we have language thinking for men. That mask must be torn from their faces. Thus is the "anti-character" comedy completed by "anti-wit" witticisms and speech-destructive speeches. [...] Once the barrier of language is disposed of, reality will assume a monstrous appearance. This is an experience reminiscent of the one Sartre describes in Nausea, only more radical.[5]

Doubrovsky's reference to *Nausea* is significant. He ties *Soprano* to a mood which reached one of its climaxes just before World War II, and the other in the decade following the war. This mood was somber, even full of despair. It is not the mood of the seventies—which on the one hand is apocalyptic and on the other millennial. Why should language communicate for men? Why oughtn't it have its own integrity and rights? Surely, as Doubrovsky says, Ionesco may have wanted to show the nothingness that lies coiled in the heart of being; or he may have wanted to deplore the subjugation of man by his former servants. Ionesco himself says, "for me, what had happened was a kind of collapse of reality. The words had turned into sounding shells devoid of meaning."[6] But we must set aside the author's intentions if we are to look freshly, more than twenty years after it was written, at a work that seems today to have relevance and liveliness. From this new perspective I discern in *Soprano* triumph and celebration—not of individualized human beings, but of the possible next phase of cultural development.

The Fire Chief and Marie are not dead like the Smiths and the Martins. They live purposeful lives; are lovers; go to fires and movies; act as servants and confessors and detectives. The Fire Chief is the man who looks for fires; Marie recites the poem, "Fire." R. D. Laing says, of fire: "There are many images used to describe the related ways in which identity is threatened. [...] The image of fire recurs repeatedly. Fire may be the uncertain flickering of the individual's own inner aliveness. It may be a destructive alien power which will devastate him."[7] Not in the usual narrative way, but in a musical and associative way the Fire Chief and Marie reinforce the major themes of *The Bald Soprano*. When Marie's fire is put out by Mr. Smith's hammer, the Fire Chief prepares to leave. "I must tell you that in exactly three-quarters of an hour and sixteen minutes, I'm having a fire at the other end of the city." The exit of the Fire Chief is the signal for the start of the final explosive dance. Marie's "death" is a prelude to rebirth—at the "other end of the city."

The two scenes which precede the dance finale (Marie's poem, the Fire Chief's exit) are more easily understood structurally than narratively. It is futile to search for meaning in the lines themselves. "During rehearsals," Ionesco recalls, "we discovered that the play had movement: in the absence of action [plot] there were actions, a rhythm, a development without plot, an abstract progression."[8] It is unfortunate that modern art took the term "abstract" as a description of a kind of nonfigurative structuring. Abstract suggests nonconcrete and general. Nothing could be more misleading. Abstract art is as concrete as the most vivid landscape and as specific as an image from one of Shakespeare's sonnets. The "abstract progression" Ionesco alludes to in *Soprano* is the movement from the finish of individuality to the assertion of a new life-force; and the dropping of all "characterization" in the drama. In most productions of *Soprano* this has led to a mechanical way of performing—as if the Smiths, Martins, Marie, and the Fire Chief were puppets. It is possible that Ionesco intended this kind of performing. Indeed, at the very long run of the first revival of *Soprano* at the Théâtre de la Huchette in Paris, it was this kind of acting that I saw. That production had Ionesco's approval, and, I believe, his assistance during rehearsals. But if a fresh interpretation of the play is possible, then maybe a fresh way of playing is called for.

NOTES

1. Eugène Ionesco. *Notes and Counternotes*. Translated by Donald Watson. New York: Grove Press, 1964, pp. 180–81.
2. Ibid, p. 28.
3. Jean Vannier. "A Theatre of Language," *Tulane Drama Review* 7, No. 3 (Spring, 1963), p. 82.
4. One of the Bobby Watsons can't even be visually "true." "She has regular features and yet one cannot say she is pretty. She is too big and stout. Her features are not regular but still one can

say she is very pretty. She is a little too small and thin." The clock is very amused by language's play and it rings five times.

5. J. S. Doubrovsky, "Ionesco and the Comic of Absurdity," *Yale French Studies* 28 (Summer, 1959), pp. 8–9. Also reprinted above, p. 11.

6. *Notes and Counternotes*, p. 179.

7. R. D. Laing, *The Divided Self.* Chicago: Quadrangle, 1960, p. 47.

8. Eugène Ionesco. *Cahiers des Saisons* 15 (1959), p. 283.

—Richard Schechner, "*The Bald Soprano* and *The Lesson:* A Lesson into Play Structure," *Ionesco: A Collection of Critical Essays.*" Englewood Cliffs, NJ: Prentice Hall, 1973.

## ALFRED SCHWARZ ON IONESCO'S THEATER

[Alfred Schwarz is Professor Emeritus at Wayne State University. He is a noted critic and scholar who has published in *Modern Drama* and *Comparative Drama.* ]

Ionesco's theater is predominantly comic because it grows directly out of his ambivalent and provocatively subjective view of the world. At first, he professes not to be able to separate comic from tragic in his experience. Wonder ... is my basic emotional reaction to the world. Not tragic all right; then comic perhaps, strangely comic indeed, derisory, this world of ours. And yet if I take a closer look at it, a kind of searing pain takes hold of me.... This type of experience is described in several places: what appears to be a strange, implausible, even nonsensical universe when viewed from the outside, in a state of detachment, causes him intense distress when he realizes that it is the sole reality of his existence. But the comic impulse prevails. Looking back upon his work, Ionesco singles out this gift of detaching himself from the world as the reason why he can view even the painful aspects of man's existence as comic in their improbability.... He is nothing if not coy in his description of the unexpected effects of his first plays upon the audiences. They laughed at *The Bald Soprano* when he thought he had written the

*Tragedy of Language*. They found the sadistic business of *The Lesson* highly amusing. Conversely, the classic vaudeville situation of *The Chairs* struck them as peculiarly macabre.... The fact is, of course, that the audiences respond precisely to Ionesco's manipulation of his ambivalent feelings in any given situation. However, his detached view is not a substitute for an objective universal view of the human predicament (such as Beckett's); therefore, he succeeds in achieving only a detached recognition on our part of his particular version of an incomprehensible universe. Since he exaggerates, or makes grotesque in other ways, the precarious nature of our existence, the audience laughs. It recognizes its image, but so enlarged or frantically distorted that it fails to share Ionesco's submerged anguish.

If indeed, as Ionesco claims, the writing of *The Bald Soprano* (*La Cantatrice chauve*, 1948; first performed, 1950) was attended by physical anguish, nausea and vertigo, why is so little of that transmitted to the audience in performance? Why does the *Tragedy of Language*, or (in Jean Vannier's more precise description) the destruction of language which ushers us into the Kingdom of Terror... make us laugh? Because his characters are so far stripped of thought, emotion, personality, having lost their identity in the world of the impersonal, that we presume to watch them from a safe distance. Ionesco writes the comedy of dehumanization. By translating the breakdown of communication into the automatic give and take of the English Language Manual, he calls attention to his detached comic view of man totally lost (or to use his own word, steeped) in his social environment. The only indication of his terror comes in the end when the tone of petit bourgeois complacency rises to a pitch of incoherent madness.... But because this typical rhythm or pattern of intensification reflects the eminently subjective response of a sensitive mentality, we feel free to stand back and laugh (perhaps cruelly) both at the comic side of his discomfiture and the grotesque expression of his terror. Ionesco's plays, as he never tires of saying, are about himself struggling to find theatrical equivalents for his own states of mind and feeling. That is really the point of his elaborate self-justifications in the *Notes and*

*Counter Notes*, as well as his speculations about the relation of comedy to tragedy.

Hence he belabors the problem of how to get from his intensely subjective apprehension of the world to a more universal, tragic vision. He declares that Beckett, in contrast to Brecht, is essentially tragic because he brings the whole of the human condition into play, not man in this or that society, because he poses the problem of the ultimate ends of man. Although Ionesco ranges himself on the side of Beckett in his concern with the authentic reality in which man is integrated ..., there is this difference to be observed between them. Ionesco does not possess Beckett's objectivity and therefore not his universality. It does not escape him that he can speak of *Endgame* in the same breath with the lamentations of Job (Job that contemporary of Beckett) or the tragedies of Sophocles and Shakespeare ..., whereas his own plays (with the possible exception of *The Killer* and *Exit the King*) hardly grasp the essentially tragic human reality ... in any universal sense. Rather they tend to fluctuate between derisive laughter at his caricatures of human behavior and sudden pain when he discovers that his invented situations accurately render his own desolation. He follows the rhythm of his intuitions and feelings instead of the logic of the invented dramatic situation. (pp. 336–39)

Beckett's comedy, on the other hand, is integral to his tragic vision. It does not compete with it (as is the case in Ionesco's tragic farce), but forms a part of the general rhythm of the play: the stalemate of *Waiting for Godot* or the descent to nothingness in *Endgame* and *Happy Days*. Nor are any of the celebrated enigmas of Beckett's drama—the identity of Godot or Clov's discovery of the small boy—evidence of his personal bewilderment or subjective expressions of his uncertainty in the face of an incomprehensible universe. Though rationally inexplicable, they are in each instance part of the objective tragic reality depicted in the play, relating to the fate of the protagonists. In fact, Beckett fulfills Ionesco's theoretical idea of tragedy, the creation of a mythical cosmos and a pure drama of universal significance that reproduces the permanently destructive and self-destructive pattern of existence itself: pure reality, non-logical and non-psychological.... But, writing in 1953, he admits ruefully, to make such a world which is peculiarly one's own communicable and identifiable to others is perhaps impossible. (p. 340)

For the most part, his talent, contrary to Beckett's, leads him to what Francis Fergusson called the partial perspectives of the modern theater, highly developed fragments of [the] great mirror. He only touches upon the tragic reality underneath the comic surface of life. The conformist, the ideologist, the purely social or sociologized man negates his humanity and thus becomes an object of derision; but insofar as in organized society man is reduced to his function in that organization, he is alienated from other men.... Concealed under the comic picture of a life emptied of meaning lies the horror of solitude. The insight is sharply realized, for example, in the automatic chatter of *The Bald Soprano* and in several other plays; but typically it has the limitations of a theatrical essay upon one of his favorite themes: that it is the human condition which governs the social condition, not the other way around.... More ambitiously, as in the masterpiece among his short plays, *The Chairs* (*Les Chaises*, 1951), he tries to deprive us of our sense of the real. The apparently harmless hallucination, begun in the spirit of vaudeville, progressively reveals the gaps in reality. The proliferation of chairs to accommodate the invisible guests suggests a more than physical absence; and at last he succeeds in expressing the void, the unreality of the real. Original chaos.... But, as he points out in *La tragédie du langage*, the tragic character does not change; he is wrecked; he is himself, he is real. Comic characters, on the other hand, are people who do not exist.... (pp. 341–42)

That the Smiths and the Martins in *The Bald Soprano* are perfectly interchangeable, because of the absence of an inner life, makes them comical in the way that puppets can be taken as abominable imitations of humanity. Accelerate their mechanical babble to the point of incoherence, and their behavior becomes painful, a kind of threatening disorder. Although Ionesco had in mind at least two explosive endings, involving the audience in a scene of mayhem, extending as it were the collapse of reality from the stage to the auditorium, circumstances forced upon him the more brilliant idea of returning to the opening scene as the curtain slowly falls. Thus the comic spirit supervenes. The Martins take the place of the Smiths, easily assuming the identity of any member of the universal petite bourgeoisie; they are people who are nothing in themselves, therefore they do not exist. The loss of identity, the absence of real people, in *The Chairs* is a decidedly more serious matter. Now Ionesco looks beneath the surface of actual existence and finds a void.... The frantic stage business, the fabricated dialogue with the absent crowd of guests—the whole grotesque effort to conceal the failure of a lifetime (perhaps of a civilization) and to push back the encroaching emptiness—inevitably breaks down. But again, face to face with the terrifying void, Ionesco truncates his statement by arranging a convulsive, farcical ending: the Old Man and the Old Woman attain their false apotheosis by leaping into the abysmal water outside, in a double suicide, and the Orator, who was to deliver the Old Man's message of salvation to the assembled guests, only gurgles and scrawls inarticulately. Ionesco's vision stops short because he is perplexed by what he has discovered; the tragic unreality of the real is a condition of chaos with which he cannot deal in a meaningful way. (pp. 342–43)

> —Alfred Schwarz, "Condemned to Exist," *From Buchner to Beckett: Dramatic Theory and the modes of Tragic Drama.* Oxford, OH: Ohio University Press, 1978.

## MICHAEL ISSACHAROFF ON THE IMPORTANCE OF BOBBY WATSON IN THE PLAY

[Michael Issacharoff is a Professor of French at the University of Western Ontario. He has been published in numerous journals such as *Romantic Review*, *Revista di Letterature Moderne e Comparate*, *Nottingham French Studies*, and *French Studies: A Quarterly Review*]

If, as some philosophers of language have argued,[2] proper names are a clear-cut instance of definite description,[3] it is instructive to examine cases in experimental drama in which the proper name does not enjoy its regular status. Most philosophers of language distinguish between at least three types of definite description: definite noun phrases, proper names, and personal pronouns.[4] Proper names have the advantage of concision, when compared to the use of descriptions that must include one or more of someone's readily recognizable attributes, and less ambiguity than the use of personal pronouns that must be linked to a speech situation, outside of which they are meaningless.[5] The function common to all three types of definite description is to identify a referent unambiguously to an addressee.[6] The Bobby Watson anecdote in Ionesco's *La Cantatrice chauve* is undoubtedly one of the best known examples of referential and naming subversion. It forms part of a systematic philosophical programme in Ionesco's early plays, particularly in *La Cantatrice chauve* and *Les Chaises*, in which the dramatist makes a parallel use of signifiers whose stability is undermined through repetition, ranging from the famous stage direction in *La Cantatrice* ('*Intérieur bourgeois anglais, avec des fauteuils anglais. Soirée anglaise ...*')[7] in which the adjective *anglais* is destabilized, to Mary's 'poem' in which the semantic status of the expression *prit feu* is jeopardized through the juxtaposition of the literal and several figurative uses.[8]

If ordinary nouns can slip referentially and semantically, thereby changing their function in a given scene, the playwright demonstrates that the so-called proper name can undergo a similar fate. In the Bobby Watson anecdote, 'Bobby Watson' is simultaneously a man and a woman, alive and dead, beautiful and ugly—a Protean creature who assumes a fresh identity in every line. In other words, each speaker determines the identity of a Bobby who has no independent existence beyond the cue that names him/her. Whereas proper names in (non-literary) speech events are not necessarily rigid designators, since, for example, places called Paris and London are to be found elsewhere than in France and Britain,[9] and likewise, there is more than one person called John Smith, nevertheless in non-playful speech situations, the use of label X to refer to person or place Y is *constant in a given context*, rather then subject to change in every sentence.

The referential consequences of the Bobby Watson anecdote are roughly as follows. Reference is scrambled through the juxtaposition of logically incompatible utterances. Scrambling is achieved through repetition of a signifier in contradictory contexts that cancel each other out. This device transforms language into an opaque mode, an end in itself rather than a means of expression, whose function is diametrically opposed to the normal role of language which is to refer beyond itself, that is, to communicate—normally through the accretion of compatible items of information. In this way, Ionesco succeeds in subverting the regular function of dramatic discourse which becomes akin to some types of poetry, particularly Dadaist and surrealist poetic discourse.[10] The other result achieved is the subversion of normal distinctions between literary genres, in this case between drama and poetry. (This perhaps accounts for the presence in *La Cantatrice* of Mary's 'poem' ('Le Feu') that she insists on reciting in honour of the Captain of the fire brigade.) Like the use of the proper name Bobby Watson, the principle underlying Mary's anti-poem is the repetition of an expression, *prit feu*, that empties it (and the poem) of semantic content and referential force.[11]

> Mon propos [wrote the dramatist] était de vider le contenu des mots, de désignifier le langage, c'est-à-dire de l'abolir. En écrivant la pièce qui s'appelle aujourd'hui *La Cantatrice chauve* (anti-pièce), spectacle qui paraît drôle et comique au public, j'avais proprement la nausée. J'essayais d'exprimer l'absence ontologique, le vide, j'essayais, c'est-à-dire, d'exprimer l'inex-primable.[12]

In fact, Ionesco somewhat understates his own practice. Rather than expressing emptiness or the void, his play, which is far more suggestive than many essays in the philosophy of language, is a primer of problems later to be explored in a rather different vein by such philosophers as Austin, Strawson, and Searle. *La Cantatrice* is a deceptive text, which *claims* to be about nothing, but which (reminiscent of Flaubert's dream of a book about nothing) is extremely rich in meaning. This is all the more surprising in a one-act play. Of course, the meaning packed into this short script is not apparent on the surface; but the playwright's insistence on non-meaning should immediately raise doubts in the mind of the reader or spectator.

A further illuminating comment by the author accounts for the comic devices in his early plays, as well as the more sombre meditation, which was to haunt him for some years, on power and language:

Faire dire aux mots des choses qu'ils n'ont jamais voulu dire.[13]

This deceptively simple observation contains the quintessence of Ionesco's philosophy of language, from the notion of identity and its presuppositions (Bobby Watson) to *Rhinocéros* and Rhinoceritis, that is, to the overwhelming power of political conformism which is contingent on the indispensable weapon of language.

A playscript can name and use names in a variety of ways, ranging from the maximum foregrounding inherent in *titles* to the mention of existents, be they persons or places. Starting with its title, *La Cantatrice*[14] names a character who never appears on stage, thus setting the tone for a universe of unreliable naming. (Fictional) titles are expected to tell us what a play or novel is 'about'. *La Cantatrice chauve* cannot be construed to be 'about' a character of that name any more than Beckett's *En attendant Godot* is 'about' a character called Godot.[15] The unreliability implicit in the title of *La Cantatrice* is compounded, at the end of the play, by the stage direction that the play should be performed over again, with the Smiths and Martins exchanging roles.[16] When the identity of the bearer of a name is not fixed, the utterances attributed to such a source are equally questionable. The dramatist, after identifying his characters with the utterances he attributes to them, turns the utterances loose, thereby destabilizing both them and the characters who speak the lines.

Naming characters and assigning snatches of dialogue is a two-way process. Naming is the dramatist's method of assigning lines on stage. The snatches of dialogue themselves particularize and individualize dramatic characters. Ionesco's strategy thus very succinctly achieves two ends: undermining the principle of naming itself—both through the Bobby Watson anecdote—and subverting all utterances by disengaging them from their speakers. As speech–act theorists have demonstrated,[17] meaning is contingent on the circumstances of utterance as well as on their being identifiable speakers and addresses. An utterance whose speaker is disengaged automatically loses its semantic and referential force.

## NOTES

2. See, for example, P. F. Strawson, *Individuals: An Essay in Descriptive Metaphysics* (London, Methuen, 1959), p. 16: 'Among the kinds of expressions which we, as speakers, use to make references to particulars are some of which a standard function is, in the circumstances of their use, to enable a hearer to identify the particular which is being referred to. Expressions of these kinds include some proper names, some pronouns, some descriptive phrases beginning with the definite article, and expressions compounded of these. When a speaker uses such an expression to refer to a particular, I shall say that he makes an identifying reference to a particular.'

3. Clear-cut, but as Gillian Brown and George Yule show, they do not have a uniquely identifying function: 'Some proper names, however, are taken to have a unique referent, regardless of context, and Plato is probably a good example. This view is extremely misleading. We might say that there is an overwhelming tendency to treat the proper name *Plato* as being used to refer to the Greek philosopher, but that contextual considerations can override this tendency. In a rather trivial way, a person can obviously refer to her child, her dog or her boat as *Plato*, given the existing socio-cultural conventions for naming entities.' *Discourse Analysis* (Cambridge University Press, 1983), p. 210. We can conclude that proper names are not necessarily rigid designators, as is sometimes claimed.

4. Oswald Ducrot, *Dire et ne pas dire* (Paris, Hermann, 1980), p. 221, adds three categories: 1) demonstrative pronouns; 2) nouns preceded by a demonstrative (e.g. this book); 3) nouns preceded by a possessive adjective (e.g. my book). John Searle, *Speech Acts: An Essay in the Philosophy of Language* (Cambridge University Press, 1969), p. 81, divides referring expressions into four categories: proper names, complex noun phrases in the singular, pronouns (e.g. this, that, etc.), and titles (e.g. the prime minister).

5. On the referential status of personal pronouns in speech acts, see especially Émile Benveniste, *Problèmes de linguistique générale*, 1 (Paris, Gallimard, 1966), pp. 251–57 and 258–66.

6. For a very clear account of these and related referential issues, see John Lyons, *Semantics*, I (Cambridge University Press, 1977), pp. 179 ff.

7. *Théâtre* I, 19.

8. The poem contains at least six distinct uses of *prit feu* (all of which can be linked to the implicit polyander with its multiple 'stems' in the first line): literal (le château prit feu), two unrelated metaphors (une pierre prit feu; les femmes prirent feu), a possible oxymoron (l'eau prit feu), a pseudo-logical use (tout prit feu) presupposing compatible antecedents, and a metalingual use (prit feu, prit feu). For a detailed analysis of the poem, see my *Discourse as Performance* (Stanford University Press, 1989), pp. 121–23.

9. For example Paris, Kentucky (USA), Paris, Ontario (Canada), London, Ontario (Canada) ...

10. Cf. M. Issacharoff, 'Le comique du discours surréaliste', *Travaux de Linguistique et de Littérature*, 25, no. 2 (1987), 163–71.

11.

> Les polycandres brillaient dans les bois
> Une pierre prit feu
> Le château prit feu
> La forêt prit feu
> Les hommes prirent feu
> Les femmes prirent feu
> Les oiseaux prirent feu
> Les poissons prirent feu
> L'eau prit feu
> Le ciel prit feu
> La cendre prit feu
> La fumée prit feu
> Le feu prit feu
> Tout prit feu
> Prit feu, prit feu.

(*Théâtre*, I, 50). The referential mechanism of the poem and the significance of the word play *polycandres/polyandres* have eluded

Ionesco specialists: thus the Watson translation, for example, an attempt to convey the spirit of the original, is not entirely accurate:

> The polyanders were glow-worming in the wood
> A stone caught fire
> The palace caught fire
> The forest caught fire
> Men on fire
> Women on fire
> Eyes on fire
> The blood caught fire
> The sand caught fire
> The birds caught fire
> The fish caught fire
> The moon caught fire
> The ashes caught fire
> The smoke caught fire
> The fire caught fire
> Caught fire, caught fire, caught fire ... caught fire ...

*Plays*, 1 (London, Calder, 1960), 114.

12. *L'Express Magazine*, January 1978, reprinted in Ionesco, *L'Homme en question* (Paris, Gallimard, 1979), pp. 186–87.

13. Ionesco, *L'Homme en question*, p. 256.

14. Using a definite noun (phrase) rather than a proper name. This is a common practice in titles of plays and novels,: cf. Molière's *Le Bourgeois gentilhomme*, *L'Avare*, *Le Médecin malgré lui*, *Les Précieuses ridicules*, *Le Misanthrope*, *Le Malade imaginaire*; Shakespeare's *Merchant of Venice*, *The Two Gentlemen of Verona*, *The Merry Wives of Windsor*; or Balzac's *La Fille aux yeux d'or*, *Le Curé de Tours*, *Le Médecin de campagne*; James's *The Ambassadors*; Hemingway's *The Old Man and the Sea*, etc.

15. Of course, the latter half of Beckett's title is 'true' insofar as his play is certainly about *waiting*. On the issue of 'aboutness' in literary texts, see my essay on the example of Maupassant's short stories, 'Phynances', *Nineteenth-Century French Studies*, 17, no. 2 (1989), 208–15.

16. *'Les paroles cessent brusquement. De nouveau, lumière. M. et Mme Martin sont assis comme les Smith au début de la pièce. La pièce recommence avec les Martin qui disent exactement les répliques des Smith dans la première scène, tandis que le rideau se femme doucement'* (*Théâtre*, I, 56). This rather significant stage direction is omitted in Donald Watson's translation of the play.

1. See, for example, John Searle, *Speech Acts*, p. 82: 'A fully consummate reference is one in which an object is identified unambiguously for the hearer, that is, where the identification is communicated to the hearer.'

—Michael Issacharoff, "Bobby Watson and the Philosophy of Language." *French Studies* XLVI, no. 3 (July 1992): pp. 272-79.

## NANCY LANE ON THE MEANING OF THE LANGUAGE IN THE PLAY

[Nancy Lane is a specialist in Twentieth Century French Literature at the University of South Carolina. She has been published in *French Forum*, *Style*, *Romance Notes*, *South Atlantic Review, and Romance Quarterly*]

A Tragedy of Language

In an important essay dating from 1958, Ionesco says that he became dizzy and nauseated while writing his first play and imagined when he was done that he had written "something like the tragedy of language" (*NCN* 179). *The Bald Soprano*, he said in a 1978 interview, was about the astonishment he felt when confronted with a world in which people talk without saying anything, or at least anything comprehensible to him, because they don't talk about "the most important thing" (death, metaphysics, the unbearable condition of human existence) (*Homme* 21). Awakened by the stock phrases and clichés of his English textbook to the emptiness of what passes for conversation, he set out to expose the mechanical, threadbare automatisms that have replaced "meaningful" language: "My plan was to empty words of their content, to designify language, to abolish it.... I was trying to find the most worn-out clichés, I was trying to express ontological absence, the void; I was trying, in other words, to express the inexpressible" (*Homme* 186–7).

The dislocation of everyday language in the play is progressive, passing through several phases. At the beginning of the play, the language is remarkable primarily for its sheer inanity. In a series of non sequiturs that might remind American audiences of Edith Bunker from the television show "All in the Family," Mrs. Smith appears to be telling her husband a variety of things he most likely already knows very well—that their name is Smith and they live in London, that they have a son and have two daughters named Helen and Peggy, that they had fish and potatoes for dinner, and so forth; the only response she receives is an occasional click of the tongue from Mr. Smith, who is reading the paper. At this point the language is empty of meaning not so much at the level of the word or the sentence but rather at the level of the entire context of the pseudoconversation. Mrs. Smith's monologue ridicules from the start the language of those who "talk without saying anything": like the dialogues in Ionesco's English textbook, her speech is pointlessly precise in stating the obvious (the children drank "English water" with their dinner, for example) and is strewn with maxims both straight ("We must teach the children sobriety and moderation") and distorted ("Yogurt is excellent for the stomach, the kidneys, appendicitis, and apotheosis").

The second stage in Ionesco's assault on language encompasses most of the rest of the play; it begins when Mr. Smith starts to speak and continues until the departure of the Fire Chief (scene 10). As soon as the monologue becomes dialogue, it is apparent that the logic governing the world of this play has nothing to do with that of spectator's world. In this part of the play, the forms of polite conversation are left largely intact, but their content is skewed and zany, much like the rapid-fire dialogue found in the movies of the Marx Brothers. A dizzying variety of techniques are used to effect this disruption of logical discourse; they include the following:

1. Pseudoexplanations. When Mr. Smith asks why the patient died and the doctor didn't, his wife answers, "Because the operation was successful in the doctor's case and it was not in Parker's" (10).

2. False analogies. Mr. Smith says that "a conscientious doctor must die with his patient if they can't get well together," comparing the doctor to a sea captain who goes down with his ship. When his wife objects that one cannot compare a patient with a ship, he says, "Why not? A ship has its diseases too; moreover, your doctor is as hale as a ship; that's why he should have perished at the same time as his patient like the captain [the French version has "doctor"] and his ship" (11). The Fire Chief complains that "production is down" in fires, and you can't import them as you can sugar because the tariffs are too high.

3. Flat contradictions. Mrs. Smith describes in great detail in her opening monologue what they had for dinner, and then, when Mary announces that the Martins, their dinner guests, are waiting, she declares that she and her husband have been waiting for the Martins and have had nothing to eat all day (14). She then tells the Martins that she didn't know they were coming, while Mr. Smith says that they had been waiting for them for four hours (20). Describing Bobby Watson (widow, wife, and fiancée of the deceased and living Bobby Watson), Mr. Smith says that she has regular features but isn't pretty because she's too fat, and that, while her features are irregular, she is quite pretty although she's a little too thin. After exclaiming that the widowed Bobby Watson is lucky to have no children, Mrs. Smith wonders who will take care of the children (12).

4. Specious reasoning. Mrs. Smith asserts that "experience teaches us that when one hears the doorbell ring it is because there is never anyone there" (23). In one of the anecdotes, a calf is obliged to give birth to a cow as a result of having eaten too much ground glass (30).

5. Surprise at the obvious. Mr. Smith wonders why the newspaper always prints the ages of the deceased and never the ages of the newborn babies (11). Mrs. Martin amazes everyone with her story of having seen a man tying his shoelaces, and her husband tops her by saying that he saw a man sitting quietly reading a newspaper, whereupon Mr. Smith exclaims, "Perhaps it was the same man!" (22).

6. Unreliability of proper names. The three days of the week when there is no competition in business are Tuesday, Thursday, and Tuesday (13). "Bobby Watson" refers to all members (whatever the gender or age) of one family, and since Bobby and his wife had the same name, it was impossible to tell them apart (12).

7. Aphasia. The Fire Chief tells of the young woman who was asphyxiated when she left the gas on because she thought it was her comb (28).

8. Contradiction between word and gesture. The Fire Chief says he can't sit down but will take off his hat while he sits down without taking off his hat (27).

Logical distortions are not the only means of "designifying" language in this part of the play. The emptiness of aphorisms and clichés continues to be foregrounded, for example, and social amenities (talking about the weather, telling pointless jokes and meaningless fables, and so on) are parodied.

The third stage in the demolition of language takes place in the final scene (immediately following the Fire Chief's exit). Now even the outward forms of conversation and dialogue are abandoned as the four remaining characters begin to hurl unconnected aphorisms and pseudoaphorisms at and past each other: "One must always think of everything"; "An Englishman's home is truly his castle"; "He who sells an ox today, will have an egg tomorrow"; "I can buy a pocketknife for my brother but you can't buy Ireland for your grandfather" (38). Phrases from Ionesco's English textbook reappear, some in English in the original: "Edward is a clerck [sic]; his sister Nancy is a typist, and his brother William a shop-assistant" (38); "Charity begins at home" (39). By this stage of the play, language has been emptied even of the appearance of being a means for conveying meaning or intentions from one character to another; rather, the characters are traversed by a flood of words and sentences that have lost their power to designate referents outside themselves. From the point when Mr. Smith exclaims, "To hell with polishing!" (39) words, phrases, and unconnected sounds, spoken in an increasingly hostile tone, circulate freely among the now undifferentiated characters until the play reaches its climax in a cacophony of violence. The sense of the individual utterances collapses as free association of sounds generates the text. This constant play between sound and sense makes the end of the play essentially untranslatable, although Donald Allen does an admirable job of trying to find English equivalents in exchanges like "Don't ruche my brooch!—Don't smooch the brooch!" ("Touche pas ma babouche!—Bouge pas la babouche!") or "Groom the goose, don't goose the groom—Groom the bridegroom, groom the bridegroom" ("Touche la mouche, mouche pas la touche") (40). Contributing to the abolition of language in the final scene are the frenzied pace of the speech, the repetition of sounds, and the sheer accumulation of words.

What Ionesco is attacking in this tragedy of language is not just certain types of clichéd social interchange but language itself. Despite a later, much more coherent style, his fundamental attitude toward language ranges from distrust to downright hostility. Twenty years after writing *The Bald Soprano*, he expressed this hostility in the following terms: "Words no longer demonstrate: they chatter. Words are literary. They are an escape. They stop silence from speaking.... Words wear out thought, they impair it" (*FJ* 73).

—Nancy Lane, "Theater of the Absurd: *The Bald Soprano* and *The Lesson*." *Understanding Eugène Ionesco*. Columbia, South Carolina: University of South Carolina Press, 1994. Pp. 31-35.

## JOHN V. MCDERMOTT ON THE MEANING OF THE PLAY

[John V. McDermott is a scholar and a critic whose publications can be found in *Explicator, Notes on Contemporary Literature, and Notes on Modern American Literature*.]

In his play *The Bald Soprano*, Eugène Ionesco objected to mundane, peripheral talk, "to diversions that tempt us to avoid thinking about or talking about the only things that really matter—the meaning of existence and the inevitability of death" (Lane 39). Ionesco was agitated because he felt that "words no longer demonstrate: they chatter.... They are an escape. They stop silence from speaking.... They wear out thought, they impair it" (Lane 35).

In relation to the idea that words no longer "mean," Mrs. Martin remarks near the end of the play "We have passed a truly Cartesian quarter of an hour" (Allen 37), which implies that those with her all knew that they existed because they were thinking. But since Ionesco parodies to the extreme their so-called thinking, they are not truly considering who they are or the reason for their existence; they are not truly living. All they wish to consider is how to pass the time as comfortably as possible.

Picking up on Mrs. Martin's inane remark, the Fire Chief incongruously blurts out the most enigmatic phrase of the play: "Speaking of that—the bald soprano?" (Allen 37). The phrase is met with "embarrassment" and dumb "silence" by the Smiths and the Martins. The silence is termed "general," for it is all-pervasive; it is not the silence that speaks. This phrase is Ionesco's happy solution to the problem cited by Coe: It is "the phrase whose very essence is meaningless insignificance but which must become significant without thereby becoming meaningful.... It must reveal its own absurdity" (48). And so it does; it is the epiphanic phrase by which Ionesco chose to reveal the complete designification of the word. In its having no connection to anything spoken heretofore, in its isolation from predication, this phrase is worse than any of the banal platitudes that have preceded it. It is the nonexistent "prima donna" that does not appear in the play, for as Ionesco said when asked why he had given the play this title, "One of the reasons ... is that no prima donna appears in the play. This detail should suffice" (177). And so it does, for the phrase which the playwright liked because of its sound signified his belief that words had become nothing but meaningless sounds.

Following the "general" silence that follows the Fire Chief's meaningless phrase, Mrs. Smith remarks, "She always wears her hair in the same style" (Allen 37). This vapid attempt at humor is not used to cover any embarrassment she may feel over her ignorance of what possible meaning the phrase may have; rather it points up her indifferent attitude toward the idea of thought, for in her world words no longer signify anything.

That "the bald soprano" was an inadvertent remark or "slip of the tongue" (Ionesco 183) by the actor who played the part of the fire chief, is an appropriate seed that must have struck Ionesco in its inappropriate relation to anything else in the play. The phrase served Ionesco's purpose well in signaling the final collapse of the word—sound without meaning, without significance—the way of the world.

—John V. McDermott, "Ionesco's *The Bald Soprano. Explicator* 55, no. 1 (Fall 1996): 40-42.

# *The Lesson*

The basic premise for *The Lesson* is the power of education amidst the dangers of indoctrination. This play has three characters: the professor, the student, and the maid, Marie.

The play begins with the maid answering the door. A student has come to the professor's house for tutoring. The maid shows her to the study. It is important to note the stage directions at this point.

Ionesco describes the girl as being a cheerful girl who is of upper-middle class status. She is lively and energetic. The rest of the stage directions explain that over the course of the play her demeanor changes, and she gradually loses her flare for life becoming more somber and morose after each interaction with the professor. She becomes much more reserved and passive.

As the professor enters the room, Ionesco uses the stage direction to give a detailed description of the professor. He is a small old man with a white beard. He conducts himself in a very professional manner; he is reserved and timid and excessively polite. Over the course of the play, he becomes more vivacious and loud, gaining confidence from the insecurity that builds in his student.

The events begin when the professor enters the room and timidly begins to apologize for keeping her waiting. He awkwardly begins questioning the student about geography, praising her excessively because she knows the capital of France. The professor is very encouraging and supportive throughout their discussion about the seasons of the year. The student informs the professor that she wishes to qualify for the "total doctorate." He initially agrees that she seems adequately prepared for the total doctorate and begins to assess her current knowledge in an attempt to design an appropriate plan for her development. At this point the first of many deviant facial expressions briefly crosses the professor's face as the student states that she is at "his disposal."

The maid enters the room walking around as though she is

looking for something. It is obvious she is checking up on the professor and as she leaves she warns him to remain calm and suggests that they don't start with arithmetic. He ignores the maid's suggestion and begins his examination of the student's arithmetic skills. He apologetically asks the pupil to tell him the sum of one and one. When the student responds correctly, he lavishes her with compliments about her intellect and superior math skills. He continues grilling the pupil with basic addition tables. The tone of the quiz begins to change when they switch to subtraction.

When the student cannot successfully solve the problem of four minus three, the professor, after being very apologetic and trying several different ways of asking her the same question, begins to lose his composure. None of his examples lead to the correct response from the student, and the insanity of the scene is further escalated when the pupil is very quickly able to calculate a nine-digit multiplication problem in her head after she had been unable to solve the simple problem. Her quick response flusters the professor, and his ranting brings the maid Marie back into the room.

Marie pleads with the professor, asking him to calm down. The professor largely ignores her as he is deeply engrossed with telling the pupil that he thinks the total doctorate is out of her reach due to her lack of knowledge in arithmetic. The professor, while still ignoring the maid who is tugging at his sleeve, decides to switch topics from arithmetic to linguistics and comparative philology. The maid's protests escalate at this point, with Marie yelling that they must not discuss that topic because "... philology leads to calamity" (Ionesco, 60).

Marie, seeing the futility in arguing with the professor, exits the room, and the professor begins a prepared lecture titled "The Fundamental Principles of the Linguistic and Comparative Philology of the Neo-Spanish Languages" (Ionesco, 60). The pupil's initial enthusiasm is quickly dowsed as the professor banters utter nonsense about the neo-Spanish languages and their origins and influences. His tirade continues until it is obvious that the student is in physical pain, complaining of a toothache.

The professor, now using a commanding and unapologetic voice instructs the pupil to quit complaining and pay attention. As the professor continues the pupil appears more and more uncomfortable, retorting to the professor's rants only by complaining of her toothache. He ignores her repeated complaints and continues in his ludicrous lecture. This scene continues on with increasing irritation from the professor and decreasing confidence in the pupil. Finally, the professor can stand it no longer and he threatens to bash in the student's skull.

The pupil is momentarily focused on his lecture again, but it is not long before she begins to whimper and complain about her toothache again. By this time the professor has begun instructing the pupil on all of the translations of the word "knife." He calls for Marie to help him find the "... Spanish, neo-Spanish, Portuguese, French, Oriental, Sardanapali, Latin and Spanish knives"(Ionesco, 72). When Marie does not respond, he leaves the dazed student, returning moments later with the maid. Hearing the complaints of the pupil about her toothache, Marie reminds the professor that a toothache is the first symptom of a condition from which other students of the professor have complained. The professor ignores Marie and begins his lesson on the pronunciation of the word knife. He forces the pupil to look at a knife while reciting "kni" followed by "fe." His voice takes on a piercing song-like tone and rhythm as the scene develops and the crazed professor continues his mad lesson. The pupil begins to complain about other ailments now in her ear, her throat, her shoulders, her breast, and her hips. In a frantic and crazed moment the professor stabs and kills the pupil.

He is noticeably shaken and dazed, and after her death seems to come out of some kind of a trance. He panics and becomes hysterical as he calls for Marie. She enters already knowing what she will find and chastises the professor, stating that this is the fortieth time he has murdered that day. He approaches the maid with the knife concealed behind his back and attempts to slash her as well, but she deflects the blow and slaps the professor calling him a murderer and a bastard. She scolds him, reminding him of her warning that philology leads to calamity. He professes that he did not understand her warning because he thought calamity was a city. The professor apologizes to the maid and tells her that he is sorry for killing the pupil. The two make the necessary arrangements for the disposal of the body. They make preparations to obtain a fortieth coffin and wreath (although the professor suggests a cheap wreath because the pupil did not pay for her lesson in advance). The two put on armbands with an insignia on them on their arms. (Ionesco suggests it may be a Nazi swastika) and the two exit the stage.

The final scene begins where the play began. There is a doorbell ring and Marie answers the door inviting yet another student in for a lesson.

# *The Lesson*

**Professor** is a man of some notoriety in the community. He is approximately 50-60 years of age. He is very soft-spoken at the beginning of the play but gradually becomes more forceful as the play progresses. Early on in the play the audience is informed that his facial expressions often suggest that he is a bit crazy.

**The Young Pupil** is an 18-year-old student who has recently finished a Science diploma and an Arts Diploma. She is attending sessions with the professor in pursuit of a total doctorate degree. She is very enthusiastic and eager at the beginning of the play but gradually becomes more passive as the lesson develops.

**The Maid** is a middle-aged housekeeper who at times treats the professor as though he is a child. Her name is Marie. She is very nervous about the professor working with the pupil and warns the professor not to teach the student philology because she fears it will lead to calamity.

CRITICAL VIEWS ON

# *The Lesson*

## RICHARD SCHECHNER ON THE HERO/VILLIAN CONFLICT IN THE PLAY

[Richard Schechner is a Professor of Performance Studies at New York University. His publication include *Environmental Theater*, rev. ed. 1995, *The Future of Ritual*, 1993, *Performance Theory*, 1985, and *Between Theater and Anthropology*, 1985]

*The Lesson* is in many ways the opposite of *Soprano*. But like so many oppositions, underlying them is an identity: for *Lesson* too is about life-force and triumph dancing. The difference is that *Lesson* uses familiar human beings.

Here, too, language is the hero/villain. Not that language possesses the Professor; no, it is his ally, his shield, his weapon, and his alibi. Truly in *Lesson* language has "metaphysical powers" and it operates like a "dissociative force exerted upon physical appearances." The knife that rapes and kills, like the philology lecture itself, is a verbal knife: a concrete being whose substance is grammatical.

Power is the X-factor of *Lesson*. When the Pupil has it, the Professor is a timid old man; when he gets it, she is helplessly gripped by numbing pain; when Marie disarms the Professor, he becomes a whining baby—but while he has the power and is strong in his rage, Marie can do nothing with him. There is just so much power, and the game/ritual of *Lesson* is the flow of this power from one to another. The power is in the language. At its deepest level, *Lesson* is a magic play, replete with special formulae and occult incantations. To know how to speak is to have power. But speaking is not ordinary English or French or any *national* language; rather, in the circularity so liked by Ionesco, the verbal language of the Professor's lecture is the worded manifestation of the language of sexual power. But this does not make of verbal language merely a mask in the debased sense of masking. No, like the Elema *hevehe* ritual, the power is the mask: without the mask there is nothing, with it everything.

The orderly transfer of power is important. It is the rhythm of the play, its dancelike repetitiveness, its circles within circles. There is no "exaltation" until all the power is concentrated in the Professor's magic knife. At that moment both the Pupil and Marie are *empty*.

Remember photos of dancers in which a torch or flashlight is carried so that after a long exposure the developed picture shows the pattern of movement? These are not motion pictures, but pictures of motion. *The Lesson* is a picture of motion and the torch is the power which flows among the three characters.

The setting does not prepare us for the play's action. There is no hint in "the office of the old professor, which also serves as a dining room" that here a rape/murder will be committed, one of an unending series. The concealment of the *insolite*[11] within the banal is a favorite Ionesco device, and part of a set of contrapuntal details in *Lesson*. Others are the Professor's age vs. his act; the Pupil's apparent innocence vs. her behavior; Marie's subservient social position vs. her control over the Professor; the seemingly passive role of language vs. its deadly power. Both the romanticism and the farce of *Lesson* come from these oppositions.

As soon as the Pupil enters, and the Professor sees her, the power flow begins. A quickly suppressed "lewd gleam" dances in his eyes. Marie, who lets the Pupil in, surely knows from experience what is going to happen. She is a sullen accomplice, a goad who guarantees the murderous outcome of events. (If *Lesson* were read as a political parable, Marie would be the "people" who seemingly deplore but actually assist each tyrant in his tyranny. The Nazi armband Marie gives to the Professor while they carry the Pupil's body out supports the political reading.) The very presence of the Pupil—young, apparently innocent, pretty—and Marie's warnings, cathect the first flow of energy.

| Latent energy | Stimulus | Obstacle | Overt energy |
|---|---|---|---|
| | Pupil enters | Marie's warning | Professor's "gleam" |

Power is expressed among the characters, and flows from one to the other. It is ideally theatrical. Finally, power is the ability to use language, "to pronounce the word knife."

Despite the Pupil's inability to answer the most simple questions, the Professor is at first very pleased with her. He sees nothing standing in the way of her getting the "total doctorate." The flirtation is obvious, and of that especially titillating kind between a very young girl and an old man. The language between Professor and Pupil is transparent, and behind it we experience the sexual play. In *Soprano* language burst through the Smiths and Martins to express its own life; here a subtext is revealed behind the text. Several times early in the play the whole rhythm of the "progressive exaltations" that make the play's action is enacted. *Lesson* is structured musically—it develops not through the revelation of plot but through the intensification and repetition of moods and patterns. These increase in intensity and widen in amplitude, are played in varying keys of anger, amusement, love, and fear.

When the Professor asks the Pupil about the seasons, when she and he sit down together, when they begin arithmetic, when he is warned by Marie, when they start philology—each of these games are properly *dances* modeled on the "scalp dance" that ends in rape/murder. These dances are sometimes introductory, sometimes titillating, sometimes climactic. It is from a musical perspective that we ought to appreciate them and to see their sexual function; it is from this same perspective that we ought to know the uses that the Professor makes of Marie's meddling and warnings which only further raise his temperature. The small reservoir of power which is teased into play at the start builds rhythmically and in waves until it possesses the Professor and overwhelms the Pupil. This wavelike, musical development can be detected in the text, but fully appreciated only during performance.

## NOTE

11. *Insolite* is a difficult French word to translate; it is one of Ionesco's favorites. It means the astonishing, the *unmaskingness* of

experience—as when the side of a building falls down to reveal your wife (or husband) in the arms of her (his) lover.

—Richard Schechner, "*The Bald Soprano* and *The Lesson*: An Inquiry into Play Structure," *Ionesco: A Collection of Critical Essays.* Englewood Cliffs, NJ: Prentice Hall, (1973): 28-31.

## Michel Benamou on Language in the Play

[Michel Benamou is a prolific critic of Modern Drama and has been published in many journals, including *Teaching Language Through Literature, The Wallace Stevens Journal, and Boundary.]*

### Philology Can Lead to the Worst

"La philologie mène au pire", warns Marie in *The Lesson*. And so it led Ionesco to write the dialogues of a college French manual. Seldom entered in check-lists, the dialogues are nevertheless of a piece with his theater. How they originated, how they function as language-learning devices and as literature, is what I have been asked to account for. This obviously puts me in a double bind, since if I say the dialogues are art, the Master (as in the Zen story) will hit me, but if I say they are not art, not worth any amount of critical attention, I shall fare no better. The way out of a double bind is to seize the stick and hit the Master with it: hence my title, which labels the message of this short note at a higher level of communication. Dialogues for a language textbook occupy in the dramatist's *oeuvre* the place of a minor genre, half-way between grammar exercises and a vaudeville skit. But then Ionesco is not merely a playwright. He is also the author of journals, interviews, a novel, children's stories, poems, drawings and screenplays. All these have to be included in the overall view.

Enter Ionesco the philologist. At the outset, the reader must be oriented to a double parody: of Ionesco by himself, of ordinary textbooks by Ionesco. Self-parody points to literary uses of the dialogues, while text-book parody has pedagogical, almost therapeutic purposes: it is necessary to revive the "victims of duty" who succumb to the boredom of language learning. To be enjoyed, the text-book parody in the dialogues presupposes a familiarity with the lethal pabulum mouthed by our students (from Latin *studiosus* pronounced *stooges*). in the so-called "audio-lingual" programs of the sixties. But of the twenty pieces we published in 1969 the best can, I think, stand on their own. The worst best, since, as the reviewer for the *Cahiers du Collège de Pataphysique* put it, "*Mise en Train* is among the best textbooks—therefore one of the worst".

When I proposed to Ionesco in May 1964 that we collaborate on a series of dialogues destined to American students, I availed myself of his attempt to learn English via the *Assimil* conversation method, which helped him to discover, if little English, at least the principle of his first play, *The Bald Soprano*. He immediately suggested a plan. There would be a fishing party, and a visit from the Parkers to the Bobby Watsons, and a tribunal scene, a carnival with fights, drunks, a two-headed woman, clowns, gingerbread and police. Would humor be allowed? He was amused, he scribbled. It reminded him of the time when he taught French at a Bucharest lycée. He wanted to know what progression I would "indicate for the difficulty and the choice of words", but he had yet to realize what an artistic challenge it would be to keep pace with the slow learning of grammar.

Language is the hero-villain of his miniature plays. If this formulation fits the larger plays so well, it describes the dialogues even better, as they mimic and parody the discourse of teachers, pedants, doctors, logicians and swimming instructors. An element of "metadiscourse" seems plain enough in *Soprano*. It originates, I think, in the teaching of language itself, since language then becomes the object of a second language, or metalanguage. Granted, this situation is not limited to classrooms. One finds it in courtrooms, pressrooms, wherever language serves to question language. But philology is pure metalanguage. The bond between literature and pedagogy is perhaps the nexus of Ionesco's method. Involuntarily in *Assimil*, consciously in *Soprano*, the dialogues are absurd because they convey next to no information. Their information dwindles to absurdity as their redundancy increases, and redundancy is bound to increase: how else can one impart, with a minimum of new words, such immortal verities as "the ceiling is above"? Ionesco used redundancy as the literary end-result of a pedagogical process. He does so in several ways. For example the characters in dialogue four, "La Soif et la faim", patiently review all the uses of the idiomatic *avoir* + noun until one of them telescopes them absurdly: "Moi, j'ai faim, j'ai chaud, j'ai froid, j'ai sommeil, j'ai vingt ans, à la fois" (*I* am hungry, hot, cold, sleepy, twenty, all at once). A language capable of such confusion must be exposed for its lack of logic, or else our lives, in which twenty years already ache as do hunger and thirst, may turn into a long tale of suffering. At the end of the dialogue, we are told it is wrong to ache all over, but it is right to need nothing. Thus the dilemma between *to be* and *to have* can never be resolved at the same level of discourse. Age is not merely an accumulation of bodily needs, even if language makes it appear so.

In his famous essay on two types of aphasia, Roman Jakobson distinguishes the ability to choose words from the ability to combine them into sentences. Aphasia results from perturbations in either function. Just as in *Soprano*, with its words gone mad, Ionesco treats the "troubles of combination" as a theme in dialogue two. Asked to make sentences out of the classroom vocabulary he has just heaped helter-skelter, a student answers: "The table is in the copybook. The teacher is in the pocket of the vest of the watch. The blackboard writes on white chalk, and the chalk erases the eraser ... I open the student and the door sits down on the bench. The bell has three schools. The book has four walls. However, the dictionary has only three windows: one English and three French windows. The windows jump out of the door" etc ... This is not really a dialogue, but an exercise whose purpose is to restore the leapfrogging words to their proper place. It shows that language can run away from people—and sometimes it can run people. Absurdity becomes a teaching device also in dialogue 9 where none of the small French shops sell any of the desired products. At the end, a melon warns us that it can be bought from two stores, a hatter's (for bowler-hats, or "chapeaux-melons"), and a vegetable stand. Then it adds an auto-cannibalistic comment: "Je me mange avec du sucre" (I eat myself with sugar). This ungrammatical use of the reflexive was surely suggested to Ionesco by redundancy, for the dialogue is devoted to too many pronominal "see" constructions. I kept it in because it is an instance of formal parallelism (il se mange—je me mange), a typical cause of funny errors in a foreigner's speech. Ionesco's dialogues touch the limits of language.

—Michel Benamou, "Philology Can Lead to the Worst," *The Two Faces of Ionesco*, Eds. Rosette C. Lamont and Melvin J. Friedman. Troy, NY: The Whitson Publishing Company, (1978): 75-77.


CHRISTOPHER INNES ON THE PHILOSOPHY OF THE ABSURD IN THE PLAY

[Christopher Innes is a Professor in the English Department at York University. His work has been published in journals such as *South African Theatre Journal, Shaw: The Annual Bernard Shaw Studies, and Modern Drama.*]

Ionesco is normally interpreted in terms of the 'philosophy of the absurd, outlined by Camus in *The Myth of Sisyphus*. His theme is said to be a statement of the impossibility of communication and the futility of life in the face of inevitable death, illustrating Sartre's proposition that the consciousness of existence leads to an awareness of 'the nothingness of being'. This is used to explain what is seen as a rejection of the whole concept of personality in the transferable or transforming characters of plays like *The Bald Primadonna* (*La Cantatrice chauve*, 1948, produced 1950) or *Victims of Duty* (*Les Victims du devoir*, 1953), the reduction of social reality to clichés and empty formulas, and an attempt to create an 'abstract' theatre where the primary function of a play is to reveal and express the formal principles of the theatrical art form. Such analyses of Ionesco's work as dramatic statements of a philosophical position, 'pure' theatre, or anti-theatre in the sense of parody drama—and given his assertion of the identity of contraries in an early essay with the title of *No!*, it would be perfectly legitimate to interpret his plays as simultaneous expressions of all three—all have a certain validity, and can be clearly derived from some of Ionesco's own theoretical statements or from selected comments about drama put into the mouths of characters in his plays. But there is a mythical, even mystical aspect to his work that is frequently overlooked, as is his relationship to the whole avant garde movement from Jarry to the surrealists. Ionesco's appreciation of grand guignol puppet theatre and his position as a 'Grand Satrap' of the Collège de Pataphysique link him to Jarry. His post-graduate thesis on Baudelaire indicates his interest in the symbolists. Surrealists like Phillipe Soupault and André Breton have hailed his work as a natural extension of their own. A play like *Hunger and Thirst* (*La Soif et la faim*, 1966), originally titled 'Life in the dream', is on one level a reworking of Strindbergian themes, with not only a structure derived from *To Damascus*, and disgust at existence symbolised as in *A Dream Play* by dirt covering the walls of a family home, but also a hero—simultaneously a Christ-figure and a projection of the author—whose pilgrimage in search of an elusive ideal in female form ends in a 'monastery-barracks-prison' where inmates are brainwashed into believing themselves to be poisoned by thoughts of freedom. And even though Ionesco rejects Artaud's theory of cruelty, he acknowledges his work to be following Artaud in his aim of creating a 'metaphysical' theatre, 'to change the metaphysical condition of man, to change life, but from within out and not the reverse, from the personal towards the collective', as well as in his attack on 'petit-bourgeois' attitudes as a 'false culture' that 'separates us from everything and from ourselves'. For Ionesco 'it is precisely the process of this devitalised culture, imprisoning us in an inauthentic reality which Artaud perceived, that defines one pole of his work, and his solution also parallels Artaud in the consequent 'necessity of breaking language in order to reconstitute it, in order to touch life, to put man back in contact with the absolute'.

From this perspective Ionesco's attack on the banality of social behaviour and the meaningless clichés of everyday language in parodies of family life like *The Bald Primadonna* and *Jack, or The*

*Submission* (*Jacques, ou la soumission*, 1950, produced 1955) take on new meaning. The pressures of conformity that have produced carbon-copy characters, whose activities and relationships are therefore arbitrary and nonsensical, are not exaggerated to reveal human existence itself as absurd, but only the forms of social conditioning that destroy individuality. 'Inauthenticity' is only contingent, not necessary. What is being attacked is the contemporary emphasis on rationality, with its accompanying materialism and devaluing of the subconscious or spiritual levels of the mind; a dualism which either produces a zombie-like vacuity, or perverts one half of the psyche into inhuman violence, as in *The Lesson* (*La Leçon*, 1951) where a professor is shown gaining total ascendency over the thirty-ninth in an endless series of pupils, which in each case leads to the rape and murder of an unresisting girl. This clearly relates to the sexual nature of power or the negation of individuality by the educational system, but on a more basic level it is an image for the domination of the intellect (in the rather over-obvious symbol of the professor) over the instinctive and physical side of human nature (the student being finally reduced to an awareness of herself solely as a body). In this symbiotic couple the Professor can only establish his dominance by repressing the Pupil's natural vitality, and the result is insanity. The point is even more explicit in *Rhinocéros* (1959), where the surface reference is political, the metaphor for men turning into rhinoceroses coming from Ionesco's personal journal of 1940 where it is specifically used to describe the dehumanising effect of Nazi propaganda. But for Ionesco politics as such is only a symptom, and he defined the play as 'mainly an attack on collective hysteria and the epidemics that work beneath the surface of reason and ideas but are none the less serious collective diseases passed off as ideologies ... concealing beneath a mask of cold objectivity the most irrational and violent pressures'.

In this light the proliferation of objects in his early plays, mounting piles of coffee cups, multiplying furniture that entombs one character, or the fungoid growth of a corpse that pushes others off the sides of the stage as it expands are not intended to represent the human condition per se, but only the effect of materialistic rationalism. The power of Ionesco's images may have made it appear that they embody an irremediable existential state, but in fact they are supposed to be a challenge to the audience, an exaggeration revealing what we commonly define as existence to be unnatural in order to provoke rejection as well as recognition, to make us aware that we are more than the empty figures representing us on stage, that there is a more authentic level of existence available to us. Hence the overt travesty in *The Bald Primadonna*, where the Martins meet as strangers and only discover that they are husband and wife by learning that they live in the same house and sleep in the same bed—yet the genesis of this situation (a game played by Ionesco and his wife on the subway) demonstrates the very capacity to care and share that the play categorically states to be non-existent—or the provocation of the original ending, where the author was to come forward and shake his fist at the audience, crying 'You bastards, I'll skin you alive.'

—Christopher Innes, "Mythic Dimensions and Modern Classics." *Holy Theatre: Ritual and the Avant Garde* Cambridge: Cambridge University Press, 1981. 202-40.


MICHAEL WREEN ON THE LOGIC OF *THE LESSON*

[Michael Wreen is a Professor of Philosophy at Marquette University. He has been published with *Philosophy and Rhetoric, British Journal of Aesthetic, Pragmatics and Cognition,* and *Philosophy and Literature*]

Ionesco begins with the methodology of logic, syntax, and focuses on arithmetic, which, we are told, "is more a method than a science" (p. 50). Since the time of Descartes, arithmetic, or more generally mathematics, has been *the* academic discipline *par excellence*, the study that all of the empirical sciences have aspired to. So completely has the idea of the mathematical nature of reality impressed itself upon us that for many people it has acquired the status of an unquestioned, and even unquestionable, assumption. And for many in this group, including the Professor, it is more than just an assumption; it is a way of life. "Let us arithmetize a little," he says to his pupil (p. 51), and his neologism refers not just to a subject matter, arithmetic, but to a way of dealing with subject matters and, ultimately, to a way of dealing with the whole of reality. The noun "arithmetic" has become a verb, and the ascendancy of abstract method has begun.

Formal logic, in all three of its classic Western forms, is now subjected to sustained and specific criticism. Generally speaking, the Pupil represents Aristotelian and Russellian humanism, a view based on an optimistic belief in man's capacity for direct knowledge, in understanding through analysis by fine distinctions between terms, and in the elimination of paradoxes, both in logic and life. The Professor, again roughly speaking, represents Hegelianism, a view based on an optimistic belief in the capacity of reason to unify a oppositions and to overcome, through a higher synthesis, the fundamentally paradoxical nature of all phenomena, including life itself. Thus, at the level of formal logic and ontology, the Professor and the Pupil are diametrically opposed, united only in their uncritical reliance upon a method of reason. This philosophical opposition is in turn correlated with a psycho-physical opposition: the Professor is male, old, retiring, and initially lifeless; the Pupil is female, young, forward, and initially vivacious. The confrontation of the two embodied philosophical/psychological principles over the matter of arithmetic makes their opposition manifest and demonstrates, for the first time in the play, the utter inability of both philosophical traditions to maintain a grip on reality.

This confrontation is also a struggle, one which the fresh, straightforward, vital Pupil begins with great success. She is "magnificent" in addition, and claims she can "count to infinity"—an ability which would vindicate her confident, optimistic belief in man's mental capacities, but an ability, nevertheless, which is logically impossible to possess, since "infinity" is not the name of a particularly large number, as she seems to think. Her claim to understand reveals her as limited and ignorant of the deeper and paradoxical nature of her subject, and thus as in need of further, more abstract lessons. "One must also be able to subtract," the Professor says, and then adds: "One must know one's limits" (p. 53). This, in fact, is just the point at which he begins to "limit" her, browbeat her into submission, make sure she knows her place as pupil.

To teach the Pupil subtraction the Professor explicates the notion of "unities in numbers," and his concept of unity, like that of Hegel, turns out to embrace the paradoxical. "Which number will be larger," he finally asks, "the smaller or the larger?" Clearly the question is tautological, and just as clearly the Pupil is bothered by its self-answering nature. Throughout the Professor's lecturing and questioning on arithmetic the Pupil is vigorously resistant, ever on the alert both for trivial tautologies and for hidden contradictions; she is ready to demand relevant distinctions and eager to expose conceptual anomalies. "In what sense larger?" and "What do you mean by the larger number?" she asks (pp. 53, 54); and as for paradoxes, she'll none of it. "The small numbers can be larger than the large numbers?" and "you are identifying quality with quantity?" she presses, with this last question clearly encapsulating one of the analyst's prime charges against Hegelianism (as well as inadvertently revealing one of the analyst's own paradoxes, namely, the *sorites*).

Continuing to behave in character, she interprets the Professor literally. To his question "What have I just said?" she answers with pluperfect accuracy, "'What have I just said?'" Her reply, however, does help to pinpoint a second fundamental concept over which the two disagree: *identity*, here construed as a formal notion applicable to everything that exists. But, as the vast literature on personal identity shows, it is very difficult to discuss *identity* apart from unity; they are conceptual Siamese twins. It is not surprising, then, to find disagreement over the one coupled with disagreement over the other, a fact readily seen as their exchange continues.

The Professor, in part as a pedagogical aid, identifies numbers with units, figures, and sticks and the student immediately pounces on him, crying Category Mistake: "One could subtract two units from three units, but can one subtract two twos from three threes? And two figures from four numbers? And three numbers from one unit?" Identifying quality with quantity is just one small mistake, it seems, just a microcosm of the macrocosm, the paradoxical notion of non-literal identity held by the Professor. And, backed into a corner, he seems to realize as much. For in response to the Pupil's barrage of questions/objections regarding figures, units, numbers, and sticks, the Professor responds with a very simple "No, miss." He is unable to explain why the answer must be No, and incapable of accounting for the seeming paradoxes, or, better, literal nonsense, of his identifications. Instead, refuge is taken in the ineffable: it is only comprehensible through internal mathematical reasoning. Either you have it or you don't" (p. 58). While the first statement here recalls Hegel's doctrine of internal relations and the role assigned to reason in his philosophy, viz., to overcome antitheses, the second functions more complexly. It is another tautology, though this time a tautology masquerading as an explanatory factual hypothesis; and it is, ironically, one of the standard examples used in deductive logic texts to illustrate Aristotle's Law of the Excluded Middle. The Professor, unbeknownst to himself, has played into the Pupil's hands.

But this is not merely a dialectical victory for the Pupil (although, supposedly, the Professor is the dialectician, not the student); it is the first explicit indication of reason, or method, twisting back on itself, betraying its own inadequacies: the Professor, the paragon of reason and, as pedagogue, of the articulate, is forced to abandon both reason and the word and to embrace the unsayable.

The Professor has now come to instantiate his own teaching. After chiding the Pupil for her "tendency to add" and her ignorance of subtraction, he explains that people "must also disintegrate. That's the way life is. That's philosophy. That's science. That's progress, civilization" (p. 55). That, in brief, is *The Lesson*'s lesson. The Pupil, unfortunately, will learn this the hard way by the play's end. As for philosophy itself, that is represented by the *Professor*—a man in whom reason tries to encompass non-reason and even anti-reason, a man in whom reason, the supreme principle of integration, integrates integration with disintegration. Such reason, however, a procedure supposedly in the service of life, more and more acquires a life of its own. That this eventually leads to the transposition of life and logic may not be evident in the early stages of the play but becomes increasingly clear as the play proceeds. As the plot develops, we see that, in the Professor's mind, life, everyday ordinary life, must conform to the method, instead of vice versa. The ultimate result of this vivification of reason is as clear as the finale of the play itself: sordid and pointless rape and murder, acts both inhuman and meaningless.

Having such a sottish, drunken-by-reason, vile intellectual pretender as a backdrop, the Pupil should shine forth. But she does not. Her initial spunk and insistence upon simplicity and literalness are refreshing, but her vitality gradually diminishes and her simplicity crosses over into simplemindedness. Subtraction is beyond her, and although she can multiply 3,755,998,251 by 5,162,303,508 in her head, and do so without pausing to take a breath, her achievement is marred by her failure to understand all questions of method. To the Professor's "But how did you know that" she replies with cheerful incomprehension, "It's easy ... I've memorized all the products of all possible multiplications" (p. 59).

The Pupil, then, is initially appealing because ebullient and clear. But she, too, is a denizen of the world of the absurd. Her stultification in the sphere of the particular (her aversion to subtraction can only stymie her efforts to acquire a "total doctorate") and her self-contradiction in the sphere of the theoretical are the paradoxes of practice divorced from reason. Its limited procedures of integration will prove ineffectual and so lead to atrophy. Opposed to these are the Professor's paradoxes of abstract reason—confusion, disintegration, and mystification in the practical sphere, literal nonsense in the theoretical. His is a reason *too* united with practice, a reason of malignant expansion. In a sense, the changing physiological conditions of the two—the Pupil gradually becoming weaker and less willful, the Professor stronger and imperious—is an objective correlative, a dramatic embodiment, of the advance of their respective philosophic diseases.

—Michael Wreen, "The Logic of Ionesco's *The Lesson*," *Philosophy and Literature* vol. 7, no. 2 (October 1983): 229-232.

# VICKY UNRUH ON LANGUAGE AND POWER IN THE PLAY

[Vicky Unruh is a Professor in the Spanish and Portuguese Department at the University of Kansas. She specializes in Latin American Theatre and the Avant Garde. She has published in *Hispanic Review, Siglo XX*, and *Latin American Theatre Review*.

*The Lesson*, first performed in 1950 in Paris, dramatizes in one act a private tutorial between a lewdly solicitous, middle-aged professor and an adolescent pupil preparing for her examinations. Despite her initial enthusiasm and self-confidence, the student gradually becomes hesitant and anxious in her responses, as the professor coaches her in geography, mathematics and philology, covering material which seems to be arbitrary, disorganized and, at times, incoherent. As the lesson gathers momentum, the student becomes less able to answer her teacher's rapid-fire questions, while the professor's agitation intensifies, despite warnings from his maid who predicts doom. While the student deteriorates from a self-assured young woman into a bundle of physical pain and devastation, her teacher is transformed from a timid and overly apologetic man into a verbal and physical aggressor. The act culminates with the professor's assault and murder of his pupil, an event charged with sexual gestures and nuance. The maid helps the professor dispose of the body, and, reassuring him about what he has done, she places a swastika—or any other comparable insignia—on the professor's arm. Addressing the audience directly, she announces that this is a routine event: the professor has disposed of forty pupils that day, and the forty-first pupil arrives as the play's opening dialogue begins again.

Athayde's *Miss Margarida's Way* was first staged in 1973 in Rio de Janeiro under the directorship of Aderbal Júnior and with Marília Pereira in the single, lead role. It has also been widely performed in Spanish America, Europe and the United States, where the playwright has worked closely with actress Estelle Parsons in developing a highly successful English version of his piece. Like Ionesco's play, *Miss Margarida's Way* is organized around a lesson, but here Miss Margarida is the teacher, and the audience is her class. As the play begins, the bell rings and Miss Margarida marches out onto the stage. Addressing the audience, she calls the class to order. The two sessions she teaches are separated by a brief recess—the intermission. Although the play's interpretation of a typical school day is dependent upon the response of the particular audience attending its performance, the written text is a relentless monologue in which Miss Margarida assaults her class with pleas, entreaties, seductive threats, provocations and confronting questions. She teaches geography, history, catechism, grammar and, above all, biology—a compendium of fatalistic observations about the human condition. Throughout the performance, Miss Margarida sends her students mixed signals. Although her goal for them is total obedience, she repeatedly tries to provoke them out of their passivity. Although she urges them to feel free to ask her questions, when a small boy from the audience walks onto the stage to ask her something, she violently sends him away. She constantly orders her students to be silent, and yet it is their mute acquiescence in the face of her verbal attacks which sends her into fits of rage, one of which culminates at the close of act two in her physical and psychic disintegration and collapse. The young boy from the audience once again walks onto the stage and revives her. Quickly recovering her composure, she informs the class that although this has happened many times before, she always revives and begins again. Gently urging her students to "do always what is good," she bids them farewell until the next lesson and departs (78). In the U.S. performance under Athayde's direction, the play ends here. In the written text, however, Miss Margarida leaves her purse on the desk, and the young boy opens it, extracting bullets and candy. After great indecision, he eats two of the candies, and, resisting the temptation to take a third, he returns somewhat sheepishly to his seat.

In both plays, traditional dramatic development and characterization are replaced by the structure of a fundamental human situation, immediately recognizable to the audience. In both plays, moreover, the nature of the relationship is initially made explicit through a variety of visual and auditory signs. In

*The Lesson*, the pupil arrives in a student uniform, carrying her satchel under her arm and casting demure last-minute glances at her homework. Her bearded teacher wears traditional professorial garb, is "excessively polite" and "very much the teacher" (46). In the opening moments of the Brazilian play, several elements suggest to the audience that Miss Margarida is their new teacher before she announces it: the bell, the blackboard, the pointer and books she carries out and lays on the desk and the skeleton she will use as a visual aid to her biology lessons. In both plays, the authoritarian structure of the student–teacher relationship is laid bare by the teachers who explain who is in charge. In *The Lesson*, the professor gives his pupil a brief pretest of her knowledge, explaining that his job is to examine her and suggesting through reinforcement that hers is to provide "good answers" (48). As the lesson progresses and the student's composure disintegrates in response to her teacher's aggression, he insists that her role is to listen, to repeat what he says in a rote fashion and to respond quickly to his questions. Similarly, Miss Margarida's opening remarks address "the importance of education" and the mutual dependence of teacher and student: "There is no good teacher without a good class" (12). Although teacher and student are interdependent, however, their relationship is not based upon equality: "let's face it, none of you is here of his own accord. You are here because your parents made you. Every one of you with no exception, right? You were all forced to come here willy nilly" (13).

In both plays, the power relationship is linked to familial and societal authority, through references to parental expectations, examinations and career requirements. The pupil in *The Lesson* is anxious to qualify for the "total doctorate," a goal in which she is reinforced by her parents and the professor who warns, in the face of her difficulties with his convoluted explanations of subtraction, of the dire implications for her future. Similarly, intolerable though it may be, school is for their own good, Miss Margarida explains to her students, and the key to the future. Class prepares for exams and the consequences of exam failure are shameful: "Failure in any of those exams is a disgrace that can mark your lives forever" (18).

In both plays, allusions to outside authorities suggest a larger societal hierarchy of which the student–teacher relationship is a part. In *The Lesson*, the maid's superior information of the situation and maternal attitude toward her employer give her an air of knowing authority. As a witness to the murders who helps the professor dispose of the bodies, she suggests tacit societal support for his crimes, and by placing a familiar insignia on his arm she stamps his activity with an ideological tone and a seal of external legitimacy: "Wait," she says, as she puts the armband on, "if you're afraid, wear this, then you won't have anything more to be afraid of ... That's good politics" (78). In her opening lines, Miss Margarida refers to the principal who had "already told me that you were a nice class", and she often invokes his name as a symbol of outside authority (12). Those who do not follow the rules, Miss Margarida warns, will be sent to the principal himself, a destination from which no student has ever returned. Although in her classroom she is the one in charge, moreover, she is angered by severe injustices she once suffered at the hands of such a director, victimized by the same authoritarian system which she now perpetuates.

The similarity of tone and structure of the power relationship in these two plays is augmented by a comparable perverse sexual dimension. According to stage directions, the professor in *The Lesson* rubs his hands together constantly with a lewd gleam in his eye. As his behavior becomes more aggressive, it also becomes more directly sexual; as his student becomes more intimidated, her discomfort is expressed in physical terms, and she complains of an incessant toothache whose pain spread rapidly throughout her body. The lesson culminates with their alternating rhythmic repetition of the word knife, accompanied by sexual gestures and sounds as the professor assaults his pupil. In the Brazilian play, Miss Margarida immediately places the relationship with her class in a sexual context by drawing explicit symbols on the board. She becomes increasingly seductive, again sending mixed signals to her students. Although she provokes their interest by launching into a strip tease and by suggesting they harbour desires she will not fulfill, she also flies into rage after rage, chastising her students for their supposed fantasies. As with the professor, behind sexual nuance and verbal abuse lies the threat of physical violence, which becomes explicit when the small boy from the audience walks onto the stage for no apparent reason. Miss Margarida asks him why he is there and suggests he return to his seat, but as he turns to go, she calls him back and performs a ju-jitsu maneuver, triumphantly pinning him to the floor. "You better learn your lesson now," she shouts as the boy flees to the safety of his seat (67). Thus, in both plays the power of pedagogy constitutes not only a form of verbal and mental control but also an ultimate threat to physical well-being.

A similar absurdist structure, based upon a repetitive human relationship of dominance and submission and containing several comparable elements, organizes the dramatic world of these two plays; nonetheless, there are significant differences in the specificity of the power relationship portrayed. Despite the presence of a swastika (which, according to stage direction, may be replaced by any other ideological sign) and despite an occasional reference to French geography, Ionesco's play creates a sense of disassociation from specifics of time and place, suggesting that such referents are fundamentally arbitrary. The professor's rhetorical statements about the weather, for example, are devoid of meaningful content:

PROFESSOR: ... What a nice day it is today ... or rather, not so nice... Oh', but then yes it is nice. In short, it's not too bad a day, that's the main thing ... ahem ... ahem ... it's not raining and it's not snowing either.

PUPIL: That would be most unusual, for it's summer now (48).

The presence of an ideological sign as a justification for mass violence suggests a twentieth-century context but without a precise national or historical referent. On the other hand, despite the fact that *Miss Margarida's Way* has been performed in many countries with specific national references changed to fit the context, it has a historical and cultural texture absent from *The Lesson*.

—Vicky Unruh, "Language and Power in *Miss Margarida's Way* and *The Lesson.*" *Latin American Literary Review* XIV, 27 (January-June 1986): 127-30.

## NANCY LANE ON THE ROLE OF WOMEN IN THE PLAY

[Nancy Lane is a specialist in Twentieth Century French Literature at University of South Carolina. She has been published in *French Forum, Style, Romance Notes, South Atlantic Review, and Romance Quarterly*]

...[T]he Professor is (on one level, at least) a contemptible, fearful tyrant, the target of satire directed at an authority (father) figure. At the same time, however, his relationships with the two women in the play establish a pattern that will continue to characterize Ionesco's protagonists—even those with whom the audience is called upon to empathize. The typical Ionesco protagonist is highly conflicted; he both desires and fears women. On the one hand, women represent erotic pleasure: the Pupil is the first of several beautiful young women who will be objects of desire in later plays (*Rhinoceros, Exit the King*, and *The Killer*, for example). On the other hand, these young women are generally unattainable, and this state of affairs leads to sadness and frustration for the hero.

Viewed from an Oedipal perspective, the Professor's desire for and hostility toward the Pupil can be read as a result of the child's sexual desire for his mother and his rage at being denied access to her body. The great majority of women who appear in Ionesco's theater are, in fact, mother figures who form a couple with the protagonist, either as spouse or as maid. These women can be nurturing and protective, as is Marie when she plays the part of "good mother," helping the childlike Professor clean up and cover up after his crime. It is she who makes it possible for him to begin his cycle anew after each murder, taking care of the details and watching out for his health. On the other hand, women are also domineering, smothering, "bad mother" figures who stand in the way of the hero's infantile desires for gratification and are thus hated and feared. Marie plays this role as well, admonishing the Professor about the dangers of continuing the lesson and reprimanding him when he once again succumbs to his desire. She is the one who holds the real power, as the end of the play reveals; she punishes the Professor soundly when he makes his one ineffectual attempt to attack her. Unable to revenge himself upon her, he will of course murder his next Pupil instead.

The Professor's misogyny is a grotesque, exaggerated version of what will be a characteristic attitude of Ionesco's later protagonists toward women. In general, they find that they both need women for the security and support they offer and resent them for the power they have to withhold gratification or to deprive the protagonists of freedom. (Perhaps the clearest example of this profound ambivalence is the two wives in *Exit the King*, one young and adoring, the other older and authoritarian.)

—Nancy Lane, "Theater of the Absurd: *The Bald Soprano* and *The Lesson*," *Understanding Eugène Ionesco*, Columbia South Carolina: University of South Carolina Press, 1994, pp. 44-45.

## DEBORAH B. GAENSBAUER ON PHYSICAL AND LINGUISTIC VIOLENCE IN THE PLAY

[Deborah B. Gaensbauer is a noted critic and scholar. She has published in *Modern Drama*, and *The French Review*.]

*La Leçon* (*The Lesson*)

When "thought is made in the mouth," as Ionesco's dadaist compatriot Tristan Tzara argued had become the norm, there is much license for satirical humor. There is also peril, as *The Lesson* illustrates. It was written in 1950 shortly after the opening of *The Bald Soprano*, at the request of Maurice Cuvelier, director of the small, underfunded Théâtre de Poche in Montparnasse, who needed a play requiring very few actors and minimal staging. When Cuvelier staged it in February 1951, the response was much the same as to *The Bald Soprano*. A friendly critic predicted:

"When we are old, we shall bask in the glory of having seen performances of *The Bald Soprano* and *The Lesson*." The public, however, stayed away from both. Those who did find their way to *The Lesson* anticipating the parodies and crumbling logic of *The Bald Soprano* were not disappointed, but they were also confronted by a more somber vision. *The Lesson* introduces the tyrannical distortions of language, physical violence, degraded sexuality, and the fascist father figure and hybrid mother-mistress-maid characters that would become increasingly familiar to Ionesco's public.

At the beginning of the play, a confident 18-year-old girl (in the dramatis personae she is designated as "the young pupil" and is typically played as very young and naive) arrives at the home of an aging, provincial professor to prepare for the "total doctorate." The lesson, which takes place in a nondescript study that contrasts comically with the startling events, soon founders. The young pupil can do addition without difficulty and can multiply 3,755,998,251 times 5,162,303,508 in an instant, because she has memorized "all products of all possible multiplications" to compensate for her unreliable powers of reasoning. She cannot learn to subtract, despite the professor's repeated efforts with imaginary chalk on an imaginary blackboard and his comically sinister warning: "It's not enough to integrate, you must also disintegrate. That's the way life is. That's philosophy. That's science. That's progress, civilization" (*FP*, 55). The pupil must settle for the "partial doctorate." The preparation launches the professor, who becomes progressively lewd and abusive, into a philology lesson as wildly distorted by preposterous facts and mangled clichés as the conversations in *The Bald Soprano*. Sounds, the professor explains, must "become filled with warm air that is lighter than the surrounding air so that they can fly without danger of falling on deaf ears, which are veritable voids, tombs of sonorities" (*FP*, 62). The fundamental principle of the linguistic and comparative philology of the indistinguishable "neo-Spanish languages" that he has promised to teach in 15 minutes, is that they are so closely related as to be "considered true second cousins. Moreover, they have the same mother: Spanishe, with a mute *e*" (*FP*, 64). There is no innocent language in Ionesco's theater. "Philology," as Marie, the professor's maid, warns repeatedly, "leads to calamity." The linguistics lesson is increasingly eroticized. "To project words," the professor informs the pupil, "sounds and all the rest, you must realize that it is necessary to pitilessly expel air from the lungs, and make it pass delicately, caressingly, over the vocal cords, which, like harps or leaves in the wind, will suddenly shake, agitate, vibrate, vibrate, vibrate or uvulate, or fricate or jostle against each other" (*FP*, 63).

The lesson degenerates into undisguised sadism as the professor comes brazenly to life, taking over language like an unscrupulous politician. Enraged by the increasingly passive pupil's agonized chorus of "I've got a toothache," he seizes a "Spanish, neo-Spanish, Portuguese, French, Oriental, Rumanian, Sardanapali, Latin and Spanish" knife (either real or imaginary) and initiates what the stage directions describe as a kind of scalp dance as the exhausted, weeping pupil moans and clutches caressingly at her body, her hand descending graphically from her neck to her stomach. His back to the audience, he stabs the girl and shudders in orgastic relief. Fending off his attempt to attack her with the knife, Marie scolds him into a state of childish contrition and takes charge of the burial arrangements. She quiets his fears that 40 coffins might arouse suspicion, assuring him that "people won't ask questions, they're used to it" (*FP*, 77). In the original version she offers the professor a protective armband like those worn by the Nazis. This gesture was eliminated by Ionesco when the play was performed. After several moments during which the stage remains empty, the maid reappears, exactly as she was at the beginning of the play, when she ushered in the now defunct fortieth pupil. The forty-first is already ringing the doorbell.

The violence is forecast by a physical metamorphosis that adds a nightmarish dimension to the humorous dialogue. The pupil, initially confident and animated, becomes increasingly morose. By the end of the play, according to the detailed stage directions, "her face must clearly express a nervous depression ... she comes to have a manner vaguely paralyzed ... almost a mute and inert object, seemingly inanimate in the Professor's hands" (*FP*, 46).

As the pupil "disintegrates," the timid old professor grows steadily more offensive until "the lewd gleams in his eyes ... become a steady devouring flame in the end" (*FP*, 46). Watching a Swiss production of *The Lesson* in which the director projected the shadows of the actors against the wall to heighten the effect of ritualized savagery, Ionesco realized that what he had at first conceived as a rape was more than that: "it was vampirism.... As the action progressed, he was devouring the girl, drinking her blood. And as he became stronger, her life was being sapped away, until in the end she was nothing but a limp rag" (Bonnefoy, 1971, 103).

—Deborah B. Gaensbauer, "Surprising Truths," *Eugène Ionesco Revisited* New York: Twayne Publishers, 1996. Pp. 64-66.

PLOT SUMMARY OF

# *The Chairs*

*The Chairs* is a tragic farce centered on the life of an elderly married couple. The entire play has only three characters: the old man, the old woman and the orator. The couple lives on a circular island that is surrounded by what the old woman refers to as stagnant water. The opening scene of the play depicts an old man approximately 95 years old leaning out of a window trying to see boats on the ocean. His wife aged 94 is trying to get him to come inside.

After much coercion the old man comes back inside. Once inside the old man is "forced" to entertain his wife by first doing an imitation of the month of February. After he performs this rather interesting trick, she then encourages the old man to tell her again, as he has told her every day of their marriage, the story of how they ended up on this island; a story that they refer to as "Then at last we arrived...." The story is more like a set of unconnected statements about an idiot, a trunk full of rice, and the rice spilling on the ground. The story is obviously very dear to the couple, but to the reader it is nonsensical.

As the old man tells the story, the old woman interjects how talented he is as a storyteller and how he is more deserving of a higher position in life. By her prodding, the old man's story and attitude changes, and he concludes that their being stranded on the island had ruined his promising career. He begins to weep uncontrollably and is consoled by his wife, who is now introduced by the name Semiramis.

She comforts her husband by telling him that he could have been anything he wanted had they remained in civilization. She treats him like a baby: he sits on her lap as she rocks him back and forth until he calms down. He is troubled by his lack of professional station in life, but feels that he can redeem his wasted life by delivering some great message to humanity. Semiramis is finally able to calm her husband down by telling him that his dreams are still attainable because they are expecting guests to arrive this evening. He lists all of the important figures who will be attending this evening: the property owners, the intellectuals, the janitors, the bishops, the chemists, the tinsmiths, the violinists, the delegates, the presidents, and many others. They are all invited to this wonderful event where an orator will deliver the old man's great message to all of humanity.

As the moment for the guests' arrival approaches the two begin to worry that the commotion will tire them out, and wonder if they can reschedule the event. The old woman desperately wants him to call off the event and her insistence causes another temper tantrum from the old man. He fidgets and wanders around the room panicking. The tension is broken with the sound of the doorbell.

Anxiously, the couple prepares themselves for their visitors, and, after leaving the stage to answer the door, they return to the room with an invisible female guest. The two politely seat the woman and enter into a very cordial conversation with her. Their delusion goes to extreme lengths as the two argue with the guest and later talk about her behind her back. They sit next to the invisible woman continuing with their small talk until the bell rings again.

The old man leaps to his feet, ordering his wife to get more chairs. He politely excuses himself from the room and exits to attend to the door. The sound of a boat departing the island can be heard in the background. As the old woman returns with yet another chair, the old man simultaneously enters with another invisible guest: a colonel. He introduces the colonel to his wife and the invisible female guest. They invite the colonel to take a seat next to the invisible woman, and the four of them begin talking. The conversation mostly centers on the colonel's ornate uniform until, once again, the doorbell rings. Both the old man and the old woman jump to their feet; the old man running to the door and the old woman leaving the stage to get more chairs for their invisible guests.

The old man enters the room again with two more invisible guests: a couple. He refers to the woman as La Belle, and it is obvious by the one-sided conversation that he has known this woman for a long time. The gentleman with her is her husband. The conversation is odd because the old man becomes fixated on how long the woman's nose has grown since he last saw her.

La Belle's husband has brought a gift for the old couple, a painting, and Semiramis is delighted with the gesture. The couple is seated next to the other two guests and they continue carrying on conversations with all the guests simultaneously. The old couple flirt with La Belle and her husband while trading cooking secrets and war tactics with the other guests. Eventually the conversation turns to the old man's relationship with his parents. He left his mother to die while he went to a dance, and he complains about suffering from this event.

As the conversation continues, boats can be heard in the background and the old couple prepare for the arrival of more guests. The old man welcomes the representatives from the press and other community figureheads as the old woman frantically moves about the room reorganizing the chairs for all the guests. This frantic process continues until the room is completely packed. Eventually, they no longer have enough chairs for all of the guests, and as they attempt to clear the aisles they are pushed violently about the stage. This continues until there is a great silence when the Emperor's arrival is announced. The couple is completely across the room from the invisible Emperor, and they feverishly try to push their way through the crowd to greet the Emperor. They finally reach the Emperor and tell him how grateful they are that he has blessed them with his presence. The old man is moved to tears as he explains how this is the highlight of his long life. Now they only await the arrival of the orator.

When the orator arrives, he enters the room very slowly. All the guests to this point have been fictional but the orator is a real person. He moves about the stage paying no attention to the old couple. The old man introduces the orator to the invisible Emperor and the other guests. As the old man addresses the imaginary crowd he announces that he and his wife have lived full lives, and that they have achieved all of their dreams. They simultaneously chant "Long live the Emperor" and both jump from the window to their death in the sea below. The moment they jump, a gasp is heard from both sides of the stage, followed by an eerie silence that is broken by the sounds of their bodies hitting the water.

The orator, who has remained silent for this whole time, now turns to face the crowd. Through hand gestures, he communicates to the audience that he is a deaf mute. He grunts, groans, coughs, offering only unintelligible sounds. He then takes a piece of chalk out of his pocket and writes ANGELFOOD followed by NNAA NNM NWNWNW V in large capital letters on the blackboard. He turns back to the audience and eagerly points at his writing. He returns to the blackboard wipes the letters off and replaces them with AADIEU ADIEU APA. He turns to the audience again with a large grin on his face in the hopes that the audience will understand him. Gradually he realizes that the audience does not understand and his smile disappears. He bows and quickly leaves the stage. After a few moments of awkward silence, laughs and coughs can be heard from the invisible audience. This noise should get progressively louder and then softer again as the real audience leaves the theater.

# The Chairs

**Old Man** is approximately 95 years old. He holds the title of General Factotum (A title that is never really explained.) He has been married to the old Woman, Semiramis, for many years. He has an important message that he wants to share with the world, and he has hired the services of a professional orator to deliver the message.

**Old Woman** is approximately 94 years old. Her name is Semiramis and she is the wife of the old man. She also acts as though she is the old man's mother, doting over him and rocking him back and forth on her lap to calm him down.

**Orator** is dressed in an artist's blouse with a loosely tied bow tie and wearing a wide brimmed black hat. He has neither the ability to hear nor speak—an occupational hazard for an orator. His lack of speech is not revealed to the audience until the old man and old woman have committed suicide, leaving the orator alone on stage in front of an invisible audience attempting to communicate the old man's message.

# *The Chairs*

## EDITH WHITEHURST WILLIAMS ON THE MYTH OF THE HERO QUEST IN THE PLAY

[Edith Whitehurst Williams is a prolific critic whose work has been published in *Folklore, Rocky Mountain Review of Language and Literature, Medieval Perspective, and South Atlantic Review*]

*The Chairs*[5] delineates the myth of the hero's quest in ironic parody. The clue to the cryptology of the play is contained in the subtitle "A Tragic Farce." Tragedy (i.e. absurdity) is not imposed upon the farcical ninety-five-year-old non-hero by an inexorable fate nor a monstrously indifferent universe, but by his own denial of his heroic possibilities. His long life, reconstructed in chaotic retrospect, follows the full cycle of the mythical quest, but hero-hood is unachieved and the old man deluded. We witness the dramatic progression of classical tragedy but see it reflected negatively, as in a mirror in which everything is reversed. The Ionesco hallmark, a proliferation of objects by which he evokes the visual image of man oppressed by an expanding mass of material things and thereby dramatizes the absence of the significant aspects of human life, is in this case the chairs; but the Ionesco theme remains the theme of human tragedy, and his ironic statement is intensified by the fact that he presents it in classical form. It is not fortuitous that the structure of the drama follows the dynamic progression which Burke has called the "tragic rhythm": action, passionate suffering, and coming to knowledge, change, redemption or restoration of order.[6] In his analysis of Burke's principle as it applies to the tragic theater, Francis Fergusson has re-stated these terms as Purpose, Passion, and Perception.[7] Fergusson's terms apply more readily to the present study as they parallel the skeletal pattern of the hero myth—*separation, initiation,* and *return*—which underlies all its variations:

A hero ventures forth from the world of common day into a region of supernatural wonder; fabulous forces are there encountered and a decisive victor is won; the hero comes back from this mysterious adventure with the power to bestow boons on his fellow man.[8]

The old man of 95 and his wife, Semiramis, 94, are first seen in a circular, sparsely furnished room in an isolated, undescribed building surrounded by darkness and water. Their almost unintelligible dialogue gradually unfolds the Purpose phase, the *separation* and crossing of "the first threshold," which is followed by defeat and unrealized strivings. The second mythic phase, the *initiation*, is normally the climactic portion of the mythical journey because it embraces the encounter with the goddess, the atonement with the father, and the acquisition of the ultimate boon, usually a message for the enlightenment of mankind. The encounter with the goddess is travestied by the old man's infantile relationship with his wife which he substitutes for the "mystical marriage" won at the price of ordeal.[9] Ionesco has selected the latter portion of this phase, preparation for *return* with a message, for his point of present action, the Passion. Whatever the undefined experiences of initiation have been, the old man is convinced of the necessity to communicate his "message." Again the pattern is inverted, for the audience has been invited to come to him, rather than his passing a return threshold to the human world; all the anguished personal involvement of the old couple is invested in their fevered preparation, as they bring in the multitude of chairs for the large (invisible) audience. "Atonement with the father" is accomplished, ineffectively, as the Emperor himself arrives and the old man attempts to justify his life with whining explanations. Atonement is followed immediately by the apotheosis—the arrival of the orator who has been hired to deliver the message. This moment takes the old man and old woman to the brink of fulfillment, and they jump simultaneously from windows on opposite sides of the room. It is a major aspect of the ironic treatment that the third phase, Perception (*return*) is denied the characters but experienced by the audience when the futility of the enterprise is made clear by the fact that the orator is mute. In Sophoclean irony the members of the audience have known the outcome from the beginning and their own guilts and anxieties are catharsized when the hero experiences his tragic defeat; in Ionesco's irony, however, the only way the tragic rhythm can move to completion is in the experience of the members of the audience who are confronted directly with the absurdity of their own inauthentic living.[10]

The author's classification, tragic farce, places the play in Frye's ironic mode:

> If (the hero is) inferior in power or intelligence to ourselves so that we have a sense of looking down on a scene of bondage, frustration, or absurdity, the hero belongs to the *ironic* mode. This is still true when the reader feels that he is or might be in the same situation, as the situation is being judged by the norms of a greater freedom.[11]

The imagery in *The Chairs* is consistent with that allocated by Frye to this mode; the "wilderness" here is a water wasteland, and the isolated, undescribed building suggests ruins. One of the earliest speeches of the old woman evokes the mood of winter, the appropriate phase of the seasonal cycle:

> There's no sunlight. It's nighttime, my darling.... I can't get used to it—Water all around us ... water under the windows, stretching as far as the horizon.

We would expect demonic symbolism rather than apocalyptic, and since the hero reflects the archetype of the hero in defeat, we recognize the archetype of the "terrible mother" in the old woman, terrible not by virtue of violence but by virtue of her capacity to debilitate and emasculate man. The symbiotic relationship between the hero who denies his own destiny and the terrible mother is well described by Jung:

> The (striving toward the) enveloping, embracing, and devouring element points unmistakably to the mother, that is, to the son's real mother, to her image, and to the woman who is to become a mother for him. His Eros is passive like a child's, he

hopes to be caught, sucked in, enveloped and devoured. He seeks, as it were, the protecting, nourishing, charmed circle of the mother, the condition of the infant released of every care, in which the outside world bends over him, and even forces happiness on him.... There appears before you on the psychological stage a man living regressively, seeking his childhood and his mother, fleeing from the cold cruel world which denies him understanding.... Not infrequently a mother appears beside him who apparently shows not the slightest concern that her little son should become a man.... You see a secret conspiracy between mother and son, how each helps the other to betray life.... He makes no more than a few impatient beginnings, for his initiative and staying power are crippled.... It makes demands on the masculinity of the man, on his ardor, and above all on his courage and resolution.[12]

The quality of the relationship is established in the first lines of the play when the old woman says, "Come my darling, close the window," and is substantiated when the old man seats himself "quite naturally" upon her lap. Meanings are conveyed by juxtaposition of words and the subsequent associations, rather than by rhetorical relationships. When the old man says, "I don't know, Semiramis, sweetheart.... Perhaps it's because the further one goes, the deeper one sinks," the sinking sensation associates with his reaction to his wife's name rather than with the logical implications of the statement. Her name in itself gives rise to some interesting conjecture in regard to symbolism. The name of Semiramis, the beautiful founder of Babylon, suggests, by extended connotation, the "Babylonian captivity" or any place of captivity. Another possibility is discovered in the fact that the same middle-Eastern queen was ultimately overthrown by her son; this reflects the non-hero's impotent desire to overthrow the devouring mother.

## NOTES

5. Eugène Ionesco, *The Chairs*. All quotations from the play are based on the Donald M. Allen translation as it appears in *Four Plays* (New York, 1958).
6. William H. Rueckert, *Kenneth Burke and the Drama of*

*Human Relations* (Minneapolis, Minnesota, 1963), p. 108.

7. Fergusson. p. 18.

8. Joseph Campbell, *The Hero with a Thousand Faces* (New York, 1949), p. 30.

9. *Ibid.*, Part 1, Chapter II, section 2.

10. Compare Rueckert's comments on *Passage to India* in which perception of reader extends beyond that of characters, p. 111.

11. Frye, p. 34.

12. Carl Gustav Jung, "Aion," *The Completed Works*, IX, pt. II (New York: 1959), p. 11.

—Edith Whitehurst Williams, "God's Share: A Mythic Interpretation of *The Chairs*." *Modern Drama*, XII, 1-4 (1969): 298-301.


## ALBERT BERMEL ON MARRIAGE IN THE PLAY

[Albert Bermel is Professor of Theatre and Drama, Lehman College. He is a drama critic and the author of *Contradictory Characters* (Dutton). He was the 1974-75 winner of the George Jean Nathan Award for drama criticism.]


*The Chairs* describes the end of a marriage. It therefore amounts to a sequel (and complement) to the play Ionesco wrote a year earlier, in 1950, *Jacques, or the Submission*, the action of which leads up to the beginning of a marriage. The pair of characters in *The Chairs*, an Old Man aged ninety-five and his wife, an Old Woman of ninety-four, open the play with some verbal sparring that sounds offhanded, if not desultory. Gradually the author transmutes the tone and narrows the direction of the dialogue, working it into and out of some masterly stage business, until the activity climbs to a feverish climax.

The old people speak of the building they are in as their home. From their description it sounds like a tower or lighthouse surrounded by stagnant water: it has the shape of a phallus, the environment of a womb. The set represents about one-half of this tower's interior. Instead of a rear wall it has a semicircular cyclorama, a construction that supports a row of ten doors and two windows. The scene thus appears to be a modified throwback to the settings for late nineteenth-century domestic farces, such as Feydeau's, in which the actors' entrances and exits (some of them more like eruptions and explosions) provide a heavy proportion of the entertainment. The rest of the stage is sparsely furnished. The playwright calls for stools below the two windows, a blackboard and a dais for an Orator, who will be coming later in the evening to address a crowd of distinguished guests, and a gas lamp that gives out a green light. (p. 412)

*The Chairs* is a memory play, the memory of a life and a marriage. But whose memory? In the text the Old Woman has almost no independent life, no story, of her own: Tell me the story.... It's also mine; what is yours is mine. Her recollections do no more than sustain or counteract his. Together they are reliving snatches of his life. She reflects and refracts him back to himself. She came into being when he was a year old, an age when infants begin to differentiate themselves from the world around them, to become self-conscious entities. Now, as an orphan crying for his mother, he takes her as a mother. When he blames life for its knocks, she substitutes for his conscience and reminds him of his faults.... (p. 415)

This married couple is a single person. It must die whole, united, as the Old Man's rhyming verse suggests when it speaks of their lying, dying, and rotting together. Yet [at the play's end] their bodies plunge separately into the water from the opposing windows. Only beyond that moment of drowning will they become one.

If the Old Woman represents the Old Man's baser self, the other live character, the Orator, stands for his higher self, the source of his message to humanity, somebody to be listened to. But the Orator must appear unreal. This higher self is a delusion, the Old Man's dream of himself magnified and elevated on a dais. The Old Man has difficulty expressing himself, but he can at least speak. The Orator, after his stunning entrance, not only cannot choke out anything but noises; when he attempts to write he deforms one of the commonest French words [adieu].

—Albert Bermel, "Ionesco: Anything but Absurd." *Twentieth Century Literature* 21, 4 (December 1975).

# ROBERT CHAMPIGNY ON FABULATION IN THE PLAY

[Robert Champigny was a Research Professor in French and Italian at Indiana University. Before his death in 1984, his works included publications in *French Literature Series*, *Symposium*, *Poetics Yearbook of Comparative Criticism*, *Stanford French Review*, *Dada Surrealism and Diacritics.*]

Designative discourse, in its engaged aspect, is taken to refer, correctly or incorrectly, to something which takes place in our historical and practical world. In its disengaged aspect, it designates something in the closed field of a game or work of art: related to our practical incarnation, what it says is not considered as either true or false. Compare what is narrated in the news, in a joke, in a children's game, in a work of fiction. In its engaged aspect, the gestural mode is used to act directly on historical persons (the speaker himself in any case) and also on historical things. The term of magic is commonly reserved for the influence of verbal and non-verbal gestures on the behavior of inanimate entities. But it could be applied to the whole range, and in particular to interhuman relations. As we pray to god, man or nature, as we beseech, request and threaten, try to coax and intimidate, encourage, depress, impress, each other and in any case ourselves, individually and in groups, we act as sorcerers.

As it is composed and interpreted, a piece of speaking or writing may emphasize one semantic mode or another. But the modes are not exclusive: after all, they draw their tools from roughly the same lexicon and syntax. If you order someone to get out, the gestural mode dominates, but the designative mode is also at work: to have practical influence, your words must refer to a historical and geographical situation. The attempt to influence carries an attempt to refer: the departure of a certain person from a certain place is intended, in both senses. Conversely, designation may be construed as the performance of an attitude which is implicitly expected to have a magic effect. Applying a causal law, even retrospectively, is to give an order to nature, and also to human beings, in any case to oneself: you order yourself to believe what you are saying. Prediction and prescription imply each other. And retrodiction involves prediction: if something has happened, it will have happened.

It is also to be noted that, whatever else we do, we cannot help incarnating ourselves historically and practically. I read a novel, I watch the performance of a drama at a historical moment in a geographical place. The experiential data are interpreted in two perspectives: as the historical performance of a drama and as a (performed) dramatic world. To the extent that the performance is successful in my eyes, I see both the actor and the character; but I do not confuse them. The pseudo-naive upholders of the theory of art as illusion make me wonder why they do not jump on stage to restrain Othello and save Desdemona. Do they equate, in this case, esthetic intentionality with sadistic voyeurism?

However, if esthetic and practical perspectives can be clearly distinguished in theory, the possibility of mixture and confusion should also be recognized. The fact that we, humans, cannot switch entirely to a playful, or esthetic, intentionality favors the confusion. Besides, it may be tempting to adopt a perspective which posits its entities as neither fictional nor historical, and yet somehow both: such confused perspectives and contradictory entities I call mythical. Performing social functions is properly to be judged from a utilitarian and ethical standpoint, which does not prevent us, if we are lucky, from enjoying playing them as dramatic roles. But we may also attempt to identify the actors and agents we are with the roles we perform, so as to escape practical fear and ethical concern. Legend is the confusion between history and fiction: we try to turn ourselves into legendary figures. And since the roles we perform, however obscurely, are consecrated, we try to confuse them with essences: the Mother, the Lover, the Professor, the Revolutionary, for instance. We pretend that our all too human city is platonically divine, that culture can absorb and redeem nature. A legendary figure should suffer only like a fictional character; and an idol is self-justified.

Narrative fiction emphasizes designation (of a non-cognitive type). Drama emphasizes gesture, verbal and non-verbal. As noted, gesture involves designation. This does not mean, however, that developing gestural meaning requires a parallel development of designative meaning. In my eyes, the main technical and semantic interest in *The Chairs*, as in some other plays of the fifties, lies in the way designative meaning, while not disappearing, is ruined and gestural meaning correlatively brought into relief. I shall examine first the negative aspect of this strategy which tends to sharpen the apprehension of the theatrical as such.

Fabulation is a traditional element where designation is much in evidence. By *fabulation*, I mean talk about what is not to be performed on stage: events before the dramatic action begins (the past of the characters, their relationships), outside events (reports of deaths), events after the end of what is to be performed (announcements of marriages; Joad's prophecy in Racine's *Athalie*). The general means of preventing designation from taking the upper hand in such instances is to motivate the report as purposeful speech within the dramatic dialectic of stimulus and response: Sophocles' *Oedipus* would provide a classical example. Apart from this, dramatists can contrive, if they wish, to lighten the designative load in various ways.

Fabulation may be eliminated: see, for instance, Tardieu's *Les Amants du métro* (*The Lovers in the Subway*). Or it may be made contradictory. By this I do not mean contradictions which are eventually resolved, errors or lies which come to be recognized as such. I mean contradictions which not only the characters, but also the spectators, are unable to resolve. Pirandello would provide illustrations, also quite a few plays in the fifties. Adamov's *Professor Taranne*, in particular, could be set in significant opposition to *Oedipus Rex*. In *Professor Taranne*, the designative load appears quite heavy if taken in suitable segments. But these segments contradict one another: fabulation cancels itself.

Stark unresolved contradictions can also be found in *The Chairs*: the two protagonists have a son and they have no children; the weather is foul and nice; the old woman does not know the colonel and has known him for a long time; the old man has let his mother die alone and his parents have died in his arms; one of the blank characters is a doctor; no, he is a photo-engraver. In this instance, however, the latter title appears to be accepted, which would resolve the contradiction. More generally, violent contradiction does not predominate in *The Chairs*. It is a limiting case which takes its place in a scale of various devices: less formal inconsistency, lack of distinction between recollection and fancy, designation turning into puns and doggerel. Rather than being set in systematic opposition, the theses collapse into fast-changing and recurring themes which, here and there, tend to be absorbed by mock-poetry. Fabulation is neutralized through dissolution.

Take the spatial and temporal setting. The old man wants to watch the boats outside in the sun. The old woman objects that it is night. The old man agrees; so the contradiction is resolved. But he adds that it is six "in the afternoon." "In the evening" would be more normal. In any case, this would mean that the action takes place in a season when days are shorter than nights. But the old man goes on to say that in the old days it was not like this: it was still daylight at nine, at ten, at midnight. At first we might think that he is confusing the seasons; but the addition of "midnight" turns possible error into fancy. Besides, the old woman does not object this time: she says that it is quite true and that he has a wonderful memory. A little later, the old man embarks upon a story: walking into a village; the name of the village was Paris, he thinks. The old woman objects that Paris never existed. The old man retorts that it did exist once, that it was the city of light (not a village) and that it flickered out four hundred thousand years ago. Rather than with contradictions, we are dealing with playful applications of the name "Paris." This kind of spirit reacts upon our original temporal assumption: that it is night outside rather than day. As far as I am concerned, it even contaminates the spatial assumption: that there are water and boats outside. True, this assumption is confirmed by mentions of water sounds. But these are only stage-directions: non-verbal indications are the actual fabulation in this case. And I see no reason why these noises, whatever device may be used to produce them, should be interpreted in a spirit different from that of the verbal fabulation. The water sounds play the theme of mutability and recurrence, thus serving as a background to the mutability and recurrence of the themes with which the protagonists play.

Consider also the pieces of information we are given about the protagonists. The old man says he is a *maréchal des logis* (sergeant) since he is a *concierge*. Thus, the military title serves only to introduce the theme of social titles, made ludicrous through the fanciful adjunct of "in chief": the old man could have been President in chief, King in chief, Orator in chief, Marshall in chief, Sailor in chief. As a *maréchal des logis*, the old man is said to have quarrelled with every marshall (in the military sense). Shall we assume at least that he is a *concierge*, in the sense of janitor, caretaker? But in the rest of the play he is always referred to as a *maréchal des logis* and even once as a *maréchal*. Besides, the job of *concierge* hardly agrees with the decor, which does not look like a porter's habitat, and with the kind of gathering which is to take place there. *Concierge* too is part of a theme: in its other sense, that of idly curious and boring gossip-monger, this word helps set the tone of the message theme.

The thesis, or hypothesis, that there is a message is not flatly contradicted: the orator's ineptitude is no proof that there is no message; the laughter at the end is no proof that a message will not be bequeathed to posterity and that the protagonists will not have a street named after them, as they prophesy. Here again, the effect of what is said regarding the message is to turn thesis into farcical theme. See in particular the caricatural evocation of literary history conceived as secular hagiography. The orator is enjoined to be a literary *concierge*: a pious biographer, he will make trivial and disgusting details appear touching and portentous.

How old are the protagonists? They have been married for seventy-five years. As a matter of fact, the way they talk might be ascribed to a second childhood. Their longevity, at least that of the old man, is quite remarkable: according to him, he did not marry before the age of forty. Still more remarkable: he was in love with one of the guests one hundred years ago. Add to this that the old woman has to juggle with chairs like a furniture mover in his prime.

They are fond of reminiscing. But their memories appear invented to illustrate themes: the sensitive child, the ungrateful son, the devoted son. One story "progresses" through puns. Another turns to uncouth free verse with a sprinkling of rhymes.

—Robert Champigny, "Designation and Gesture in *The Chairs*." *The Two Faces of Ionesco*, Eds. Rosette C. Lamont and Melvin J. Friedman. Troy, NY: The Whitson Publishing Company, (1978): 156-161.

## Elizabeth Klaver on the Use of Language in the Play

[Elizabeth Klaver teaches advanced courses in modern drama, drama theory, media studies, literary theory, and postmodernism at Southern Illinois University-Carbondale. She has been published in *New Theatre Quarterly*, *American Drama*, *Mosaic*, *Essays in Theatre Etudes Theatrales*, and *The Journal of Popular Culture*]

The critical method of The Chairs becomes similarly privileged, and lies as well in the transformation of a condition into dramatic action and structure. The proliferation of chairs on the stage is the major, ongoing, dramatic event, but the chairs also mark absence, creating the condition of showing what Ionesco has, at various times in *Notes and Counter Notes*, called the presence of the absence, the ontological void, the invisibility of characters, the absence of real people, and spiritual absence. As in *The Lesson*, the critical method turns into the plot or rhythm of the play, for we are no longer looking at just the condition of absence, but at the very way absence informs the play, creating dramatic action in the fictional world by the proliferation of absence, and in the responses of the old couple to it, from their dialogue to their suicides. Illusion, absence, and the ontological void gain as much power, enough even to kill, as the disembodied word.

Moreover, the play foregrounds its own critical method in the way the chairs mark not only the presence of absence, but also in the way they mark the absence of language itself. One semiotic system is used as a foil to the foreground, and through its presence oppose, the emptiness of the other. As Ionesco notes, "the theater has its own idiom: a language of words and gestures and objects, action itself." Semiotic systems "speak" in their own manner, and in this case, one can be said to speak about the other. Indeed, "absence can only be created in opposition to things present," by juxtaposition with another semiotic system.

Yet the absence of the language is also emphasized by the presence of language. Because the chairs can mark and give direction to the emptiness, one-sided conversations can proliferate in the play when the old couple engage in discussion with the "chairs"; as noted above, sometimes these "dialogues" break down utterly, for the absence of the other side of the conversation creates gaps in the audience's understanding. On the other hand, when the conversation is more than mere verbal notation, the one-sided conversation often seems to make more sense than the dialogue between the old man and the old woman. For example, the reminiscence of Paris the old couple share becomes incomprehensible:

| OLD MAN AND | (*laughing together*) At last we laughed. |
| OLD WOMAN | Ah! ... laughed ... arrived ... arrived ... [...] the |
| | idiotic bare belly ... arrived with the rice ... |
| | (p. 481) |

Yet, the juxtaposition of monologue/conversation between the old man and the invisible Belle, and between the old woman and the invisible photo-engraver, actually produces quite a bit of sense, understandable by the audience even to the point of recognizing that the old man's romantic lovemaking is being set off against the old woman's wantonness. The use of language is much more complex than seen in *The Bald Soprano* or *The Lesson*, for rather than just witnessing the linear progression of the emptying of words by cliché and slogan or the gradual development of power through discourse, *The Chairs* hovers back and forth between the absence of language generating sense or generating nonsense in all types of conversation present in the play.

However, regardless of whether the audience is capable of gathering meaning in spite of the missing parts of the dialogue, the absence of language always produces the condition of linguistic gaps. In this way, we are once again looking at the critical method whereby the stage is filled, because language is absent, with more and more gaps in language (represented by empty chairs), producing certain dramatic actions such as the mixing up of the gaps- failing to apply the appropriate speeches to the appropriate identities:

| OLD WOMAN | I'm suffering from liver trouble, Doctor, Doctor! ... |
| OLD MAN | This gentleman is not a doctor, he's a photo-engraver. (p. 492) |

Or they perceive the gaps as barely differentiated labels:

| OLD MAn | My wife ... Mr. ... Mrs. ... my wife ... Mr. ... Mrs. ... my wife. (p. 497). |

The absence of language thus becomes internalized into the dramatic language and action, producing not only gaps of meaning, but also affecting dramatic events for the "real" characters, who try to fill the linguistic gaps with their own conversation, generating for themselves the belief in an "audience."

The attempt to fill the gap of language with language becomes a fundamental quality of the play. The chairs point to both the absence of language and the presence and growth of the ontological void. As Ionesco puts it, "this vacuity [should] slowly invade the stage, continually covering up, with words used like clothes, the absence of real people, the gaping holes in reality." Words try to cover the holes and yet are part of the holes; language tries to cover its own absence by filling up the void, yet the void tends to empty the language by producing holes in the discourse. The language which is present keeps trying to turn the absent language into something by displacing it with invisible, imaginary people and their conversation, yet the absence of the language undermines this process by continually producing ever larger gaps which must be covered by tropes. As the abyss on stage grows larger, the ability of language to produce tropes becomes compromised, for it can't keep up with the emptiness that eventually takes over.

This play within the ability of "present" language to cope with absent language, indeed the play between presence and absence in general, goes right to the heart of the play's ontology. As Derrida notes, the history of the "matrix [of metaphysics] ... is the determination of Being as *presence*," a fundamental center of presence which is beyond play, and which is renamed with various metaphors: *eidos, arche, telos, energia,* etc. With the critique of metaphysics by Nietzsche, Freud, and Heidegger, the notion of presence as a center disappears, and is eventually replaced by the notion of a play of differences, the traces of presence and absence. The fundamental sense of being in *The Chairs* is informed by a solid, metaphysical "presence," so that the naming. or troping, which takes its form from this kind of ontology, has an inherent play of differences within itself, an inherent wavering between states of being.

This play of differences shows up as a basic equality of words themselves in *The Chairs*. As in *The Lesson*, where the word is foregrounded as it gathers powers and strikes, in *The Chairs* the words are foregrounded in their basic, linguistic form. Throughout the play, but especially towards the end, language is often produced from slight conceptual, associative and/or acoustic variations. For instance, when the old man addresses the Emperor, the old woman echoes his language:

| | |
|---|---|
| OLD MAN | ... thanks to the usher ... |
| OLD WOMAN | *(echo)* ... usher ... rusher ... |
| OLD MAN | ... His Majesty the Emperor ... |
| OLD WOMAN | *(echo)* ... jesty the Emperor ... |
| OLD MAN | *(in a total silence)* ... |
| | A little silence...Your Majesty ... |
| OLD WOMAN | *(echo)* ... jesty ... jesty ... (p.512) |

These slight changes in sound not only demonstrate the basis of our differentiation and understanding of words, but also point to the traces of what is "not said" in the near repetition, a fundamental aspect of signification; furthermore, they generate new meanings in the text, producing in this case parody or irony.

The play of differences is also fundamentally at work in the presentation of characters, in the indeterminacy over what constitutes "real" entities. The oppositions carry the traces of each other in themselves, for we can always catch a glimpse of the "other" as it threatens to come into existence and dominate what seems to be present. For instance, we are kept wavering constantly between wondering if the chairs indicate imaginary people or nothing, or if the "real" characters are imaginary and the imaginary characters "real". Ionesco is no help:

> Why can one see the Orator and not those other characters who crowd upon the stage? Does the Orator truly exist, is he real? Answer: he exists neither more nor less than the other characters. He is as invisible as the others, he is as real as unreal, neither more nor less.

In fact, this play of differences is so vast and pervasive that even when we linger in the acceptance of character marked by the chairs, there are more than one, two, or three possible assignments of identity. To displace nothing, we are offered the presence of the Colonel, Mrs. Belle, the photo-engraver, the Emperor, and numerous Mr.s, Mrs.s, and Misses. Even the "real" characters become a play of differences, showing the traces of what is "other":

| OLD MAN | I've invited you...in order to explain to you... that the individual and the person are one and the same. [...] |
| | I am not myself. I am another. I am the one in the other. (p. 503) |

Given this kind of discourse, with its constant play of differences, what impact does it have on its own world-creating properties and on the kind of dramatic world generated? Language, along with set, actors, costumes, gesture, etc., is one of the semiotic systems used to create the dramatic world, helping to bring it into existence through self-referring statements. As Elam notes, "In the absence of narratorial guides, providing external description and 'world-creating' propositions, the dramatic world has to be specified *from within* by means of references made to it by the very individuals who constitute it." An important type of self-reference is deictic language, which speakers use to refer to themselves, their listeners and their spatio-temporal situation. It is "one of the principal means of putting entities into the universe-of-discourse so that we can refer to them subsequently." In *The Chairs*, much of the deictic language is referring to entities which are neither invisible or non-existent. For instance, the Old Woman says to the invisible colonel, "This chair is for you ... Sit here, please" (p. 489) indicating both a listener and a spot in space. At times, the deictic information becomes very complex as the old couple refer to many "invisible" entities and spots in space almost simultaneously:

| | |
|---|---|
| OLD WOMAN | Who are all these people?... May I introduce you, excuse me ... May I introduce you ... but who are they? |
| OLD MAN | May I introduce you ... Allow me to introduce you ... permit me to introduce you ... Mr., Mrs., Miss.... Mr. ... Mrs. ... Mrs. ... Mr. (p. 498) |

By pointing at things and their spatial-temporal position, the deictic language helps generate a world of invading, "invisible" entities.

—Elizabeth Klaver, "The Play of Language in Ionesco's *The Chairs*" *Modern Drama* XXXII, 4 (December 1989): 521-527.


ROSETTE C. LAMONT ON TIME, AGING, AND VISITORS IN THE PLAY

[Rosette C. Lamont is professor of French and Comparative Literature at Graduate School and Queens College, City University of New York. Her publications include essays in *Massachusetts Review, Modern Drama, Grand Street, and Nottingham French Studies*. She has also published a book on Ionesco called *Ionesco's Imperatives*.]

*The Chairs* presents an aged couple (the Old Man, 95 years old, and the Old Woman, 94 years old), living in complete isolation in a building surrounded by water, a watchtower or lighthouse. The Old Man, the "janitor" of this tower, calls himself Quartermaster General. His wife entertains him in the illusion that he is a man of genius who might easily have become president, doctor of medicine, or field marshal, had circumstances beyond his control not turned him into the failure that he is. The Old Woman is both wife and mother to her husband. She rocks him in her lap, fondles him, sings him popular songs, lullabies, and blows his nose when he gets weepy. When he whines that he is motherless, an orphan—Ionesco suggests that we never forget the loss of parents we loved, that time does not heal—his wife whispers that she is now his mamma. As he lies limply across her lap, we are presented a cartoon version of the Pieta.

Having played the mother role, the Old Woman turns into a respectful wife. She encourages her husband to tell her a story she has heard a hundred times but, much as children do, enjoys listening to all over again. Now it is she who plays the role of a small child, one who needs to be pacified.

Ionesco draws for his audience a devastating picture of dependency. He does not spare any of the grim details that render marriage an association of two helpless, self-indulgent, egocentric individuals, who try to find in each other their own image and the comfort they lost in growing out of childhood. However, his protagonists are in the state of second childhood; they have come full circle.

Time in *The Chairs* is some kind of vague future; the landscape suggests a catastrophe that might have annihilated most of the planet, drowning the mainland under some gigantic tidal wave. The Old Man tells the Old Woman the story of a great city of which nothing remains save a popular tune: "Paris Will Always Be Paris." The title is in itself an ultimate irony since obviously Paris has disappeared. In fact, so much time has elapsed since the city's annihilation that the Old Man is no longer certain whether this place called Paris was a small village or a great metropolis. It was known, he recalls, as "la Ville Lumière" (the city of lights), but this light was extinguished "four hundred years ago."

Nothing has survived, not even ruins as in Persepolis. The destruction seems as complete as that of the great pyramid of the mysterious Pharaoh Radedef at Aby Rawash. The glorious capital of France, the jewel of the world, has suffered the fate of Carthage and Byzantium. No doubt Ionesco's audience recalled with a shudder the Germans' master plan to blow up their city before retreating, as they did in Warsaw. Paris came close to being nothing more than a dot on a map.

With the game of story telling over, as well as that of sipping imaginary tea from invisible china cups, a new subject is introduced by the Old Woman, Semiramis. The old hag is endowed with a grotesquely ill-suited name, that of the Assyrian princess who supposedly founded Babylon. The ancient name may go with her wrinkled face and mummylike body, but it emphasizes the passing of a glorious epoch. However, the Old Man and his wife have kept a sense of history, a desire to leave a trace of their passage on this earth. Since they cannot build pyramids or plan suspended gardens, they will turn to oratory, that off-shoot of philosophy that flowered as a conscious art from Gorgias to Aristotle. Since the Old Man is no Demosthenes, he wonders whether he will be able to acquit himself of this task. His admiring, tirelessly supportive wife tries to build his self-confidence. Her comment furnishes us with the perfect illustration of one of Ionesco's typical stylistic devices: the seemingly throwaway line enclosing a key concept, indeed an aesthetic principle.

> It's easy once you begin, like life and death. It's enough to have your mind made up. In speaking, ideas come to us, words, and then we, in our own words, we find everything again, the city, the garden. Then we are no longer orphans.

Ionesco starts with a joke: What is easy about "life and death"? Then we recognize the writer who likes to quip: "I write to find out what I think," the dramatist who dictates his plays to a secretary, writing them as he speaks. The passage culminates in a moving praise of the art of oratory and of writing. Through this activity we find what was lost in the depths of our memory: "the city, the garden." Better still we encounter our dead parents, our relatives, and friends. "Then we are no longer orphans." Thus, the Old Woman's injunction is also the writer's statement about the nature of his art. Ionesco, who always says that he cannot imagine for himself any other life than the one of man of letters, says that it is in literature that as readers and writers we find our true home.

Because the Old Man is full of self-doubt he will take no chances: he has invited a professional orator to deliver his message. Like the ancient Greeks, he believes that "the orator" is the prose artist par excellence, the one able to make the *written* word *heard*. For this momentous occasion a great crowd has been summoned. Ionesco draws up one of his absurd lists held together not by meaning, but by rhyming words, alliterations, rhythmic patterns. Since there is no rhyme or reason for this grouping of people, the effect is of a chaotic mob.

> The property owners and the intellectuals ... the janitors, the bishops, the druggists, the tinsmiths, the violinists, the delegates, the presidents, the police, the merchants, the buildings, the pen holders, the chromosomes ... the post office employees, the innkeepers, the artists ... the proletarians, the clerks, the military, the revolutionaries, the alienists and their alienated.

It is a mad hodgepodge of opposites, of people and objects, much like the "production" line in *The Future Is in Eggs*.

The guest list drawn, a sound is heard outside; a boat glides through the water, comes to a stop at the bottom of the lighthouse. This sound is followed by a doorbell ringing. The Old Man and his wife rush out of one of the many doors at the back of the stage. They can be heard speaking to someone in the wings. Slowly, they back into the room, talking with animation to their first visitor. Finally, they separate, allowing the guest to pass. This is the moment when the audience realizes that all the visitors will be invisible, imaginary.

The first invisible guest is a woman. The space she is imagined to occupy is framed by her excited hosts. The Old Man walks out to fetch an extra chair since, at the start, there are only two downstage. In the meantime, the visitor and her hostess occupy these two. When the Old Man returns, he sets his chair on the other side of the empty one, the guest's chair.

Soon the bell rings again. From this time on there will be a steady flow of new arrivals. The Old Man rushes to open the door, while his wife fetches the chairs. Her comings and goings become so precipitous that it is hard to imagine that the same person is performing all the exists and entrances. Tsilla Chelton, who was a young woman when she played the role, achieved the speed of an automaton, a marionette gone wild. Her act echoed the comical assembly-line scene of Chaplin's "Modern Times." No wonder; Ionesco stated a number of times that his sources must not be sought in dramatic literature but in the circus, the cabaret, and above all silent films. He jokes in all seriousness: "I belong to the cabaret school of drama. My ancestors are Charlot [Chaplin], the Marx Brothers, the Keystone Cops, Buster Keaton, Laurel and Hardy, and the cartoon characters, Les Pieds Nickelés." Tsilla Chelton is a clown in this tradition. Tall, gaunt, made up to look ashen, she literally ran in breathless circles behind the set to reappear almost instantly upon disappearing. She created the visual illusion that there were two of her on the stage at once. It was an unforgettable tour de force as breathtaking as watching an acrobat walking a tight rope. She lived up to Bergson's definition of the comic in *Le rire*, "le mécanique plaqué sur du vivant" (something mechanical superimposed on something alive). Exhilarating and comical, her performance captured the very essence of Metaphysical Farce.

As the stage becomes peopled with an invisible, yet not inaudible crowd (Ionesco calls for sounds that suggest a room filling up with people), empty chairs are placed in neat rows, their backs to the audience. The effect is of another theater orchestra, the mirror image of the real one below. Clearly the "show" is to take place upstage, where a huge double door dominates the back wall. Meanwhile, the Old Woman, who has become an usher, circulates up and down the aisle selling popsicles, candy, cigarettes, and cold drinks, just like the *ouvreuses* in French movie houses.

All of a sudden the doors at the back soundlessly swing open. A hush falls over the room as the Old Man and the Old Woman stand petrified, awestruck at the apparition. It is the supreme moment of a lifetime: the Emperor, as invisible as the rest of the guests, has arrived.

The audience in the theater is caught in the magic make-believe of the moment; yet, instantly a cruel realization dawns on the public: nothing has actually happened, there is no one there. The Emperor's entrance is part of a dream, or a rehearsed game played by the couple on many of their solitary evenings. This time, however, it is an endgame.

—Rosette C. Lamont, "Metaphysical Farce." *Ionesco's Imperatives: The Politics of Culture.* Ann Arbor, Michigan: The University of Michigan Press, 1996. 72-76.

## ELI ROZIK ON STAGE METAPHOR IN THE PLAY

[Eli Rozik is professor of Theatre Studies at Tel Aviv University. He has been published in *Journal of Pragmatics, Theatre Research International, Semiotica, and South African Theatre Journal*]

In the elliptical forms of metaphor, including stage metaphor, the improper predicate describes the object of predication (the subject of the sentence), such as a character, not by means of its literal meaning, but by means of other predicates (verbal and non-verbal) arrived at by an associative process. The assumption is that the improper predicate, after setting in motion an associative process, which eventually evokes a predicate that makes sense on the literal level, stops being part of the description and can be ignored. For example, if we say that 'the old man is a baby', the intention is not that the word 'baby' is a permanent component of the description of 'old man', since in such a case it would be false: he is not a baby in any literal sense. In fact, 'baby' ceases to be a predicate after producing associations such as 'splashes', 'mumbles' and 'sobs'. Metaphor thus implies that the improper predicate is negated as a literal predicate: the metaphor 'is a baby' literally means 'is not a baby'. Metaphor is not false, it is improper.

In addition, metaphor implies that only the associations of 'baby'—such as 'splashes', 'mumbles' and 'sobs', including non-verbal associations originating in 'baby'—are the active and proper predicates of 'old man'. In the case of an explicit metaphor such as 'the old man sobs like a baby' the same rule applies: only 'sobs' and its non-verbal associations originating in 'baby' are the active predicates of 'old man'. In other words, the old man can sob like an old man (literal predicate) or sob like a baby (or any other improper predicate). Since there is no difference between the literal 'sobs' and the metaphorical 'sobs' which is mediated by the improper term 'baby', we may conclude that the latter evokes an alternative source of non-verbal associations.

On the structural level there is no difference between verbal and stage metaphor: they feature the same syntactic and semantic qualities. The difference resides in the media. In the theatrical medium the verbal metaphor 'the old man sobs like a baby' is produced by an actor enacting both an old man (indicated by signs such as wrinkles, shaky walking and cracked voice) and sobbing in a way characteristic of a baby. Both sets of signs, the literal and the improper, are imprinted on the body of the actor. These verbal and stage metaphors reflect, however, the same structure and the same semantic components, and should thus be viewed as equivalent, the same metaphor in two languages. It is natural, therefore, that stage metaphors are sometimes described by verbal metaphors in stage directions, as I have demonstrated elsewhere.

Another difference, which also derives from the nature of the medium, resides in the fact that verbal metaphor features an improper word while stage metaphor features an improper image (or iconic sign). Whereas in both cases, after setting in motion the associative process, they become superfluous, it might be the case that a word can be more easily ignored then an imprinted image. Otherwise we cannot understand why a theatrical style that features stage metaphors in abundance is so difficult for the audience, whereas verbal metaphor in dialogue is less obstructive. The reason could be that the actor, who produces both the images that derive from literal description (old man) and the images that derive from an improper description (baby), give the impression that all these enacted indices of a given character enjoy the same degree of 'reality': all are literal. This could be the reason for the sense of absurdity that texts indulging in stage metaphors create, particularly if they activate simultaneously various sources of associations which are improper to each other. This impression is, however, erroneous, since literal and metaphorical indices should be 'read' differently. Moreover, since metaphor is a means of description, this apparent absurdity is a feature of the text and should not 'contaminate' the fictional world. The fallacious tendency of the audience is, however, as illustrated by the Theatre of the Absurd, to ascribe improper terms of stage metaphors to the fictional world, making this style inaccessible to the wider public. This fallacy is also reflected in the current theoretical approaches to this type of drama.

—Eli Rozik, "Stage Metaphor: With or Without. On Rina Yerushalmi's Production of Ionesco's *The Chairs*," *Theatre Research* 19, 2 (Summer 1994): 148-156.

# *Rhinoceros*

Eugène Ionesco's best-known play, *Rhinoceros* is an absurdist play mocking conformity. The play is one of Ionesco's few pieces of work that contains more than one act. It is composed of three acts and four scenes, the events of which take place in a provincial French town in the district of Little Castille. The main character is Bérenger and the events of the play center around his emotional battle with conformity.

The play begins with two characters, Jean and Bérenger, meeting at a café. Bérenger is a bit of an alcoholic and Jean criticizes him about his lack of social grace in regards to his appearance and his obvious alcohol problem. The two discuss Bérenger's lack of punctuality and direction in life, but everything is interrupted when a charging rhinoceros rambles through town causing a housewife to drop all of her groceries. The townspeople are obviously shaken and disturbed by the event. Jean and Bérenger continue their conversation about Bérenger while periodically referring to the oddity of the charging rhinoceros. While they talk they are on stage next to the logician and the old gentlemen, whose conversation becomes intertwined in their own. The logician and old gentlemen are engrossed in a philosophical conversation about syllogisms. As their discussion develops there is a noise heard off stage and once again a rhinoceros charges through town in the opposite direction as the first.

While the townspeople have a considerably more casual reaction to the charging rhino the second time, the cat of the housewife is trampled by the rhino, and it takes a great deal of comforting and a snifter of brandy to calm her down. A heated argument ensues between Jean and Bérenger about whether the second rhino was in fact the same rhino as the first one that ran past. Everyone in the cafe becomes involved in the discussion. Jean claimed the rhino that just ran by was a different rhino from the first because the first rhino had two horns, making it an Asiatic Rhino, while the second only had one horn making it an

African Rhino. Bérenger does not agree and tells Jean that the rhinos passed by so quickly and with such a great rustling of dust that it was not possible to determine the number of horns on the animal(s). Jean persists in his argument, and Bérenger informs him that his rhinoceros knowledge is in fact incorrect, and that the Asiatic rhino only has one horn while it is the a African that has two. This debate continues until everyone in the cafe is huddled around Jean and Bérenger waiting for the argument to escalate into a physical confrontation. The scene ends when Jean leaves the cafe.

Act two begins at a government office where Daisy, Bérenger, Dudard, Mr. Boeuf, and Botard work together. The scene opens with Dudard, Botard, Daisy and Mr. Papillion talking. Daisy is trying to convince Botard that she really saw a rhinoceros the other day. Botard, thinking that this is some clever ploy against society, scrutinizes her even though Papillion and Dudard mention that they have also heard about the rhinoceros sightings. The conversation escalates with the arrival of Bérenger who confirms Daisy's story. Botard remains unconvinced. The conversation ends with Papillion ordering everyone to get back to work. As they return to work Mrs. Boeuf enters the office out of breath to inform Papillion that her husband is sick and will not be at work today. When she is questioned about why she is out of breath, she explains that a rhinoceros chased her all the way down the street. As she finishes her explanation a rhinoceros is heard downstairs trumpeting and running into the wooden staircase that leads to the office, eventually destroying it. Through the following conversation, it is revealed that the rhinoceros in this case is actually Mr. Boeuf after he has transformed into the animal. In a bizarre scene, Mrs. Boeuf leaps from the balcony, landing on the back of the rhinoceros and the two ride away.

The second scene of act two takes place in Jean's apartment. Bérenger goes to Jean's house to see how his friend is feeling. Jean's appearance is rather disturbing to Bérenger, and Bérenger wants to call the doctor. Jean has a bump on his forehead that grows larger throughout the scene; in addition, his skin gradually becomes green and rough. He is turning into a rhinoceros, and by the end of the scene, he completes his transformation and tries to attack Bérenger.

Act three opens in Bérenger's bedroom, which bears a striking resemblance to Jean's. Bérenger is tossing and turning in his sleep. He is having a nightmare about the rhinoceroses that have taken over the town. He is awakened from his sleep by the arrival of Dudard. The two men discuss Jean's recent transformation, Dudard explaining to Bérenger that Bérenger is not at fault for what happened to Jean. Bérenger is excessively worried that he may have contracted what the two call rhinoceritus. Given that Bérenger was present during Jean's transformation, he is preoccupied with the idea that rhinoceritus is an air-born agent, and he too will change into a rhinoceros. The two deduce that the best protection against the epidemic or rhinoceritus is will power, and as long as they are determined not to contract the virus, they have nothing to worry about.

The conversation turns to the repairs of the destroyed staircase at work. Dudard states that the wooden staircase was replaced with yet another wooden staircase instead of a stone one. Then the conversation turns to Papillion's sudden retirement. Dudard maintains that Papillion has retired until Bérenger questions the reasons for his retirement. After Bérenger questions Dudard at great length, Dudard finally confesses that Papillion did not retire but rather has also turned into a rhinoceros. Bérenger is shocked and disturbed by this most recent transformation, but Dudard seems to think that the rhinoceroses have a peaceful natural appeal. He continues to explain how becoming a rhinoceros is not all bad and reveals that even the logician turned into a rhinoceros. Bérenger becomes irate at this point and begins screaming to the passing rhinoceroses that he will never join up with their kind.

After a few minutes Daisy enters. She has come over to see how Bérenger is doing since he has not been at work for a few days. She informs Dudard and Bérenger that Botard has recently made the transformation. Her attitude is very nonchalant about the event. She describes Botard's change as a willing transformation with his last words being that he must go with the changing times. Daisy and Dudard talk about the benefits of becoming a rhinoceros while Bérenger continues to discuss the superior status that humanity has over the rhinoceroses. Eventually Dudard, in an attempt to make an informed decision about which is better, decides that he cannot choose until he has experienced both. Dudard leaves to try out the rhino lifestyle, and Bérenger and Daisy are left alone.

The rhinoceros noises coming from outside grow gradually louder and take on a kind of musical quality as more and more people become rhinos. Bérenger and Daisy are left alone in Bérenger's room. Bérenger professes his love for Daisy and he repeatedly describes how their way of life as humans is far better than anything the rhinoceros movement can offer. The two discuss how good their lives together will be, and the two gradually become more relaxed until the phone rings. It is the rhinoceros crowd trumpeting into the receiver. They are both very frightened. Bérenger is unable to see any redeeming quality in the rhinoceros crowd, and he lashes out against their cause.

Bérenger is still adamant about remaining human, but Daisy is beginning to waiver. She does not see the use of fighting against the crowd. Bérenger suggests that he and Daisy will have to become the modern day Adam and Eve and begin to repopulate the Earth with humans; however, Daisy is not convinced, suggesting that maybe it is the two of them who need to change. Bérenger is outraged at this suggestion and slaps Daisy. He tries to apologize, but the rhinoceros sounds have taken on such a beautiful melody that Daisy leaves Bérenger to join the rhinoceroses. Bérenger is still opposed to the group mentality and tries to plug his ears with cotton to avoid their siren-like song. He storms around his room screaming at the rhinoceroses. He stares at himself in the mirror trying to convince himself that humans are better than rhinos primarily because they are better looking. Eventually he begins to question how attractive he or any human is. He takes out pictures and examines them. The longer he stares at the pictures the more grotesque and less familiar the people in the pictures become. Eventually he determines that humans are actually ugly, and that the rhinoceroses are very beautiful. He is now ashamed to be human and tries to will the transformation to occur. After several attempts to induce the transformation he concludes that he is meant to be human and that he will have to fight against all of the others. The play ends with Bérenger screaming, "I'm the last man left, and I'm staying that way until the end. I'm not capitulating."

# *Rhinoceros*

**Jean** is a very neat and socially aware individual. He is constantly arguing with Bérenger about his appearance and his drinking problem.

**Bérenger** is the main character in the play. The character of Bérenger is thought to be a fictionalized version of one of Ionesco's friends who eventually became a Nazi supporter during WWII. Bérenger is very carefree at the beginning of the play. He seems to have no sense of time and is constantly late for engagements with friends and for work. He has a drinking problem that is the source of much ridicule from both his friend Jean and from the woman he loves, Daisy.

**The Waitress** is a diligent worker in the café in the first act. She is charged for every dish that breaks as the rhinoceroses roar by the café.

**The Grocer** spends a great deal of time in act one looking out the window at the people walking by. He is the first to rush out when the housewife drops her bags when the rhino charges by.

**The Grocer's Wife** also spends a lot of time staring out the window. She bad-mouths the housewife as she walks by claiming that the housewife is very snobbish and acts as though she is too good for the grocer's store.

**The Old Gentleman** wanders around in the first act spending most of his time listening to the logician. When he is not in deep conversation with the logician he is making passes at the housewife.

**The Logician** is obsessed with only analyzing issues from a logical point of view. He is a classical philosopher using the primary idea of a syllogism as a manner of interpreting the universe.

**The Housewife** is a woman of fairly high social status. She is walking by the café when a rhinoceros charges by. The first time it rushes past she drops her groceries but manages to hold on to her cat. The second time it runs by she drops the cat, and the cat is trampled to death by the rhinoceros.

**The Café Proprietor** has only one concern: making money. He charges the waitress for every plate that is dropped. He is very greedy and cares little for the feelings and/or well-being of others.

**Daisy** is the woman that Bérenger loves. She works in the same office as Dudard, Bérenger, Botard, and Mr. Papillon. She is in her twenties, blond and very attractive.

**Mr. Papillon** is the head of the Department where Bérenger works. He is about forty years old and astutely dressed with a large brown mustache.

**Dudard** is about thirty-five years old and during the play he wears a gray suit with black sleeves on to protect his clothes. Tall and slender, he is energetic and a dedicated worker. He and Botard do not get along.

**Botard** is a former schoolteacher. Stout and arrogant, he will not admit to being wrong about anything. He is about sixty years old and wears a beret most of the time.

**Mrs. Boeuf** is a large woman. She is only in the play for a brief period. She comes to tell Mr. Papillon that her husband is ill and will miss work.

**The Fireman** is a dutifully civil servant who rescues Daisy, Bérenger, Dudard, Botard, and Mr. Papillon when the stairs are destroyed by one of the rhinoceroses.

**The Little Old Man** lives at the end of the hall near Jean's apartment. His name is Jean as well and he answers the door when he hears Bérenger calling for Jean in the third scene.

**The Little Old Man's Wife** is a character who is never seen on stage—only heard.

**And a lot of Rhinoceros Heads**

# *Rhinoceros*

## ROY ARTHUR SWANSON ON COMPARING BÉRENGER TO ORESTES

[Roy Arthur Swanson was a professor at the University of Wisconsin-Milwaukee in the English and Comparative Literature department. He published numerous essays in journals such as *Utopian Studies, Germanic Notes, World Literature Today, and Science Fiction Studies.*]

The focus of the trilogy is Orestes' act in the interest of justice. On one side of this act there is darkness, savagery, entanglement, and injustice. These negative elements are balanced, on the other side of Orestes' act, by light, docility, disentanglement, and justice. The effect of the trilogy as a whole is not of progression but of balance. When we center our attention upon the umbilicus of the trilogy, we are presented, not with the succession of darkness by light, but with the tense equipoise of light and darkness. In the human world the most that can be done in the interest of justice, or in the quest for justice, is to balance the good and the bad. This balance is implicit in Orestes' act, which is good because it avenges a wrong and bad because it is matricide. The absurd paradox is the commission of evil in the interest of good: the means are not justified by the end; it is the reverse: the means justify (make just) the end. In the same mode, Clytemnestra (evil) gives birth to Orestes (good); good is a product, not a justification, of evil.

We take note that in *Rhinoceros* Ionesco reverses the Oresteian pattern of animal imagery; he develops a proliferation of rhinoceroses. The reversal of pattern is not an essential change in dramatic structure; it is no more than a variation in usage. The play opens with one rhinoceros in a world of humans and ends, after Daisy's exit, with one human (Bérenger) in a world of rhinoceroses. The tragic balance between the worlds of non-conformity and conformity is achieved in classical Greek dramatic fashion but with humorous instead of grave effect. There is no definite movement from non-conformity to conformity; what we get is a rhinoceros-hided exposure of stultifying conformity as a changeless mean.

Leonard C. Pronko offers a deft comment on Ionesco's classical balance: "While *Amédée* begins with a feeling of oppression, heaviness, and opacity, and ends with the euphoria that is described metaphorically by Amédée's escape into the night sky, *The Killer* begins with an evocation of the radiant city in which all men seem destined to be happy, and ends in darkness, silence, death. The décor of the first act is suggested by lights, brightness, clarity; it seems a spring day. The last act shows us twilight, dusk, the nightfall of man's life." We may add that one changeless mean, namely, the ignorance of reality and unreality, is common to both plays.

Of the thirty-one extant Greek tragedies those that begin happily end unhappily, and those that begin unhappily end happily. In each the effect is that of balance, not of progression; and the movement in each is regularly toward a restoration or resumption of balance. The Greek audience would attend, not merely to the conclusion of the tragedy, but to the total work; it would leave the theatre with a perception of beginning, middle and end; the middle, so perceived, would emphasize or define the balance of beginning with end. One of the functions of the choral stasima was certainly to contribute to the audience's experience of stasis. John Bull gives humorous depth to this function in (= *A Stroll in the Air*). Greek tragedy presents the paradoxes of human life, those ridiculously unreasonable or incongruous factors which inform human life. A tragic hero comes into an awareness of these factors, and his audience is made to experience and sustain this awareness. Absurdity is bearable so long as its incompatible factors are recognized as such and are held in balance. Donald Watson, in the "Retrospect" to his translation of *Amédée, The New Tenant*, [and] *Victims of Duty* (New York: Grove Press, 1958), speaks of the "dynamic tension" of Ionesco's world: "a world in which the familiar and the unfamiliar, the logical and the illogical coexist but never correspond." Tension is the life of balance in Greek tragedy and Ionescan drama.

As an absurdist, Ionesco, like Beckett, establishes precisely that kind of balance which is manifest in Greek tragedy. The absurdist's balance is achieved by frustrating the actions and desires of characters, or by immobilizing characters and events, or by running actions and events in snake-swallowing-tail cycles. To the stasis of balance the absurdist playwright adds the element of humor as *une autre face du tragique*.

Ionesco's *Unhired Killer* (or, *The Killer: Tueur sans gages*) and Pinter's *The Dumb Waiter* are like the *Oresteia* in their presentation of the inevitability of killing. Aeschylus underscores the absurdity of killing as a necessary means of combatting killing. The denominator common to the act of injustice (the killing of Agamemnon and Cassandra) and the act of justice (the killing of Clytemnestra and Aegisthus) is the killing of a man and a woman. The difference between the two acts of killing lies only in their respective motives. In the Ionesco and Pinter plays the element of differentiation (motive) has been removed: killing, despite its inevitability, can be assigned no meaning whatsoever. In Greek tragedy the possibility of assigning meaning to actions and events is realized. In absurdist theatre the possibility exists but is not realized. In both forms of drama it is clear that meaning is arbitrary and gratuitous in view of the facts that it *can be assigned* and is therefore not absolute.

Greek tragedy regularly establishes a context of assigned meanings: *hubris* is destructive; killing indiscriminately or with ulterior motives is unjust; *aretê* is ennobling; etc. Humor is inappropriate to such a context. Absurdist theatre disestablishes contextual meaning, and actions and events become merely ridiculous; they become humorously tragic. They become so tragic that they are funny, like those in Stanley Kubrick's *Dr. Strangelove* (as compared, say, to the American filming of *On the Beach* or the Russian filming of *War and Peace*). They become tragicomic. In Ionesco's radiant city, Bérenger's ineptitude is comic (Chaplinesque, Kafkaesque, etc.); it is also tragic—not now-comic-and-now-tragic, but indissolubly comic *and* tragic. The antics of Pinter's Ben and Gus, as they strive to fill the orders from above, are tragicomic.

The theatre of the absurd is the theatre of humorous tragedy. It is drama in which the absurdity of human life, long ago recognized by the Greek tragedians, is seen for what it is and occasions laughter. Le Roi Jones' play, *The Toilet*, and Michael McClure's play, *The Beard*, are not absurdist: the tragedy which they touch upon is upheld by shock, violence, and sensation, but not by humor. Albee, Beckett, Grass, Ionesco, Pinter, and Simpson rarely fail to evoke the humor of tragedy. They and playwrights like them have given us the genre of absurd drama. If Jones, McClure, et al., have any historical antecedents, those antecedents must be Seneca, Hrosvitha, Kyd, and the Shakespeare of *Titus Andronicus*. The antecedents of the absurdists are Aeschylus and Sophocles.

Ionesco's *The King is Dying* (or, *Exit the King: Le Roi se meurt*), for example, is as Sophoclean as Anouilh's *Antigone*. Anouilh has written a "black play" which serves as a tragedy that defines tragedy: "[...] the conqueror, already conquered, alone in the midst of his silence [...]. Tragedy is honest. It is calm and certain [...]. There is tranquillity in tragedy [...]. Guilt is a matter of assigning roles! One person kills, another is killed, according to the role in which he is cast. Above all, tragedy is restful because it assures us that there is no longer any hope, foul hope." Anouilh's *Antigone* is Sophoclean because it *expresses* the nature of Sophoclean drama. Ionesco's *King* is Sophoclean because it *reflects* the nature of Sophoclean drama. Anouilh's *Antigone* is not absurdist, as the *King* is: the *Antigone* is quite without tragic humor. The tragedy of Anouilh's Creon is not humorous; that of Bérenger I is very humorous.

The state ruled by Bérenger I and the state of his being are synthesized as the state of ignorance in a skillfully constructed pun on "l'État, c'est moi." Bérenger I takes note of his ignorance by saying that he is like a schoolboy who takes an examination without having done his homework, like a *comédien* (actor) who does not know his part on opening night, like a speaker who is led to the platform without knowing the first word of his speech or the character of his audience: "I do not know these people. I don't want to know them. I have nothing to say to them. What a state I'm in!" The guard announces that the king has made a reference to his state; and Marguerite comments, "Dans quelle ignorance." Bérenger I then rushes to the window to cry out to the people, to the world, that he is going to die, that he must die; but no one pays attention.

The Bérenger of *Unhired Killer* (= *The Killer*) and the Bérenger of *Rhinoceros* are both aware of their own ignorance and are both frustratingly confronted with ignorance of ignorance. No one in the radiant city is ready or willing to stare death, the irrational killer, in the face. Bérenger alone, in the concluding scene, converses with the implacable killer. He faces the nothingness of death and recognizes the absurdity of life. In *Rhinoceros* Bérenger again stands alone. He is as ignorant of the force represented by the rhinoceros-disease as his *Killer* counterpart is of the force represented by the irrational killer. At the same time, each Bérenger is as aware of, respectively, the killer and the disease as he is ignorant of the forces inherent in them. At the conclusion of *Rhinoceros* it is Bérenger's awareness of his personal ignorance which prevents his becoming a rhinoceros, even though he could be disposed to become one.

A historical model for the Bérenger of *Unhired Killer* (= *The Killer* [1959]) might be Alphonse Marie Bérenger (1785–1866), the great lawyer who made a career of advocating reforms in criminal law and seeking the institution of criminal rehabilitation. A fitting model for the Bérenger of *Rhinoceros* (1960) could be Bérenger de Tours, a non-conformist theologian (c. 1000–1088), whose concerted attacks on the doctrine of transsubstantiation won him the condemnation of the high church, to which he managed never completely to capitulate. The Bérenger of *The King is Dying* (= *Exit the King* [1962]) may call to mind Bérenger I, king of Italy (898–924) and emperor of the West (915–924), who was assassinated at Verona. But the literary model for all of these Bérengers and for the Bérenger of *The Walker on Air* (= *A Stroll in the Air* [1963]) is best identified as the Sophoclean Oedipus, who learned that he did not know, intensified his awareness of his not knowing, and then became the patriarchal teacher of those who did not know that they did not know. This is the movement of Sophocles' Theban cycle, with its extremes of *hubris* and *aretê*; and it is the movement of Ionesco's Bérenger cycle, with its changeless mean of ignorance.

In his use of animals as effective symbols of ignorance, Ionesco is, again, like Aeschylus, whose Oresteian world of darkness (ignorance) is infused with the animal imagery we have noted. Ionesco equates the killer with people's indifferent ignorance of the killer by having Bérenger call him monkey, tiger, mule, hyaena, and cur. The rhinoceros, likewise, represents both ignorant conformity and the state of being unaware of ignorant conformity. There is, incidentally, a striking parallel to animalism-as-ignorance in Matthew Arnold's citation of Joseph Joubert: "Ignorance, which in matters of morals extenuates the crime, is itself, in intellectual matters, a crime of the first order." He goes on to refer, figuratively, to "our implacable enemies, the *Church and State Review* or the *Record*,—the High Church rhinoceros and the Evangelical hyaena." William Inge's motion-picture scenario, *All Fall Down*, outlines the fatal effects of noncommunication that is symptomatic of ignorance; the disease and its cause are united in the central figure, a willfully indifferent rake named Berry-Berry (cf. beri-beri, and seeds or fruit of destruction) and nicknamed "the old rhinoceros."

The imagery of ignorance in *The King is Dying* (= *Exit the King*) is Sophoclean again. Ignorance is manifest in the death-counsel given the king by his two wives and his doctor. Bérenger I appears initially as a headstrong, youthful Oedipus. The very first physical indication of his moribund condition is the pain in his legs. Like Beckett's Oedipal Estragon, he has foot pains; and he limps. When the Tiresian doctor tells him that he is to die, he behaves at first with the same impatience and outrage that Sophocles' Oedipus directs to Tiresias. Gradually Bérenger I accepts the fact of his death, but not without rebellion and an increased love of life. As he stares death in the face and resists death by living as fully as he can, he achieves a superiority to his two wives and his doctor, each of whom tries vainly to inject scientific or philosophical meaning into the king's death. But science and philosophy are ultimately no more than disguises of the facts that life is life, that death is death, and that every living man is mortal. The king sees through the disguises and, like Oedipus disappearing among rocks, he fades away in a mist.

The doctor is a surgeon and a bacteriologist; but he is also an astrologist and an executioner: science cancels itself out in its inevitable service to quackery and death. Marguerite and Marie, the two queens, serve death in their respective attempts to reconcile death with life. Juliette, the maid and nurse, serves death by failing to see the sublimity of life in even the most menial tasks, Bérenger I alone refuses to serve death. The others, who think they uphold the spirit of man by their various interpretations of literal life, are no better than the guard, who takes everything literally. Juliette says that life is not pretty ("La vie n'est pas belle"), and the king answers, "It is life" ("Elle est la vie").

Sophocles' Oedipus and Ionesco's Bérenger are both, to use a worn-out but accurate phrase, everyman figures. Both are toppled from presumption to a painful awareness of the essential unhappiness and absurdity of human life. Both are conquered by the mystery of death after tenacious resistance to death and futile struggles to solve its mystery, which tenacious resistance and futile struggles are not obscured by ignorance of death's irresistibility or by the futility of struggle.

The Bérenger cycle holds up life as death's joke. Ionesco's antidote to the fear of death is laughter at its joke. Black comedy makes jokes about death, but it does not show that life is death's joke; moreover, its true character, like that of sick comedy, is unabashed tastelessness. The "theatre of cruelty," whose chief practitioners are Antonin Artaud and Jean Genet, exposes the sickness of conventional morality; it does not present everyman caught up in the ridiculously humorous struggle of life against death. Death's joke on everyman is a prime subject of Ionescan theatre, which sets the tragicomic pace of the theatre of the absurd.

—Roy Arthur Swanson, "Ionesco's Classical Absurdity. *The Two Faces of Ionesco*." Eds. Rosette C. Lamont and Melvin J. Friedman. Troy, NY: The Whitson Publishing Company, (1978): 130-136.

## G. Richard Danner on Bérenger in the Play

[G. Richard Danner is professor emeritus at Ohio University in the Department of Modern Languages. He has published in *French Review and Kentucky Romance Quarterly*]

In the first place, it must be made clear that Bérenger is not a spokesman for any real-life notion of humanity, nor is Ionesco's version of rhinoceritis a pragmatic phenomenon suitable for the research projects of social scientists. *Rhinocéros*, like any significant literary work, does offer its audience an implied analogy with human experience. But analogy is never identity. Bérenger exists only in the text. He has no knowledge of the struggles of the individual in our society; he is unaware of our martyred minorities, the tyranny of technology and bureaucratization, brainwashing, and governmental policy formulated in defiance of accountability to the public. Those who insist on treating Bérenger as an advocate of a historical concept of humanity must decide at the outset which concept they will have him defend and which collective threat they will have him attack. Since the play does not answer these important questions, partisans of this approach to literature find themselves free to mold Bérenger like a lump of soft modeling clay: Bérenger the anti-fascist today; Bérenger the anti-Communist tomorrow. Who knows? We may soon be asked to consider Bérenger as the Lillian Hellman of French theater, however great the ontological distance between the events described in *Scoundrel Time* and the action of *Rhinocéros*. Playing the parlor game of pin-the-parable-on-the-personage may be intellectual fun, but as a substitute for critical method it is a pastime too undisciplined to be illuminating. Literary criticism and sociology are both respectable avenues for coming to terms with certain kinds of reality, but they are governed by different rules and they are further distinguished by separate definitions of what is real. Since Bérenger's reality is contained by the play, it is the play alone that we must consult in order to determine what the notion of humanity might mean to Bérenger and to those around him.[8]

From the outset we find little in Bérenger's life that would appear to be worth defending. Early in act I he confesses to his friend Jean that he is bored and tired and unsuited to the office job that he nonetheless performs dutifully eight hours every day—minus vacations (p. 12). Alcohol is his vehicle for escaping the monotony of this daily routine. Drinking helps him not to be afraid. It relaxes him and allows him to forget. Jean, betraying the mental vacuity that will be one of the play's constants, poses as amateur psychologist by advancing a ready diagnosis: "C'est de la neurasthénie alcoolique, la mèlancolie du buveur de vin" (p. 23). But Bérenger seems to ignore this interruption. His dilemma, like those of other Ionesco characters, finds expression in images of heaviness: "Je sens à chaque instant mon corps, comme s'il était de plomb, ou comme si je portais un autre homme sur le dos" (p. 23). This feeling prompts him to doubt that he is who he thinks he is. But the bottle enables him, so he claims, to shed the sensation of added weight and to reclaim his lost selfhood: "Dès que je bois un peu, le fardeau disparaît, et je me reconnais, je deviens moi" (p. 23). Yet for him the process of becoming himself involves no real choice, commitment or even self-acceptance. Latter-day Chatterton as bureaucrat, Bérenger laments, "Moi, j'ai à peine la force de vivre. Je n'en ai plus envie peut-être" (p. 24). Bérenger, as hopelessly maladjusted as Lord Byron's Childe Harold but lacking the solace of the Romantic hero's communication with nature, exclaims, "La solitude me pèse. La société aussi" (p. 24). He seems to harbor a death-wish—"C'est une chose anormale de vivre" (p. 24)—but the author has chosen not to provide him with that standard stage prop of the age of Victor Hugo: a vial of poison. Since Bérenger has failed in his own life to achieve a full and rewarding sense of humanness, we should not be surprised to discover that he does not manage to plead the cause of humanity persuasively or even coherently when pachyderms replace human beings as the norm in his world.

The other characters in the play are no more successful than Bérenger in creating, through their lives, a form of humanity that would appear worth struggling to preserve. Consider Jean, for instance. Why does he, as Bérenger believes, have strength of character? "D'abord, j'ai de la force parce que j'ai de la force," Jean reasons weakly, adding, "Ensuite j'ai de la force parce que j'ai de la force morale." He claims, finally, "J'ai aussi de la force parce que je ne suis pas alcoolisé" (p. 24), yet he will turn down an invitation to accompany Bérenger to the theatre that evening precisely on the ground that he must meet some friends at a saloon. This is of course no proof of a serious drinking problem, but it at least suggests, in the context of his earlier remarks, that Jean has a confused and contradictory mind. Such a lack of coherent reasoning may suffice, in Jean's own opinion, to deny the nonthinker's very existence, for as he says to Bérenger, comically paraphrasing Descartes, "Vous n'existez pas, mon cher, parce que vous ne pensez pas! Pensez, et vous serez" (p. 25).

If meaningful thought is the necessary criterion for being, the Logician (who has a minor but memorable role as the master of the false syllogism) is perhaps less alive than anyone on stage. Confidently ignoring the logical limits of his premises, he concludes that four-pawed creatures are necessarily cats. Someone has a dog with four paws. "Alors," the Logician intones peremptorily, "c'est un chat" (p. 24). By toying with his terms the Logician can even cast Socrates in his feline farce: "Tous les chats sont mortels. Socrate est mortel. Donc, Socrate est un chat" (p. 25). To be human here is to be free to use faulty rhetoric as an instrument of intellectual anarchy. One can imagine Voltaire, whose literary armies foolishly slaughter each other in attempts to control a pile of mud, laughing loudly at anyone who would lift a finger to protect the humanoid quagmire pretending, in *Rhinocéros*, to be the human race.

It is a mark of Bérenger's lack of discernment that he is favorably impressed by the Logician, calling him "une personnalité distinguée" (p. 96). Ironically, Bérenger slips into a syllogism of his own when the visual evidence strongly suggests that the Logician has been transformed into a rhinoceros. Bérenger's syllogism can be reconstructed as follows. The Logician wore a straw hat when last seen. A rhino appears wearing a straw hat pierced by its horn. Therefore the beast is the Logician. Though the play does not destroy this hypothesis, the argument contains a fallacy based on the possible existence of a second straw hat or the transfer of the Logician's hat to someone else (by loan, sale or theft); but these possibilities are never explored.

## NOTE

8. The source of all references to *Rhinocéros* in this essay is Eugène Ionesco, *Théâtre*, III (Paris: Gallimard, 1963). Page indications are parenthesized in the text.

—G. Richard Danner, "Bérenger's Dubious Defense of humanity in *Rhinocéros," The French Review*. 53, 2 (December 1979): 209-211.

## DAVID BRADBY ON LANGUAGE IN THE PLAY

[David Bradby is a Professor of Drama and English at the Royal Holloway, University of London. His work has appeared in such journals as *New Theatre Quarterly, Franco British Studies, Nottingham French Studies, French Cultural Studies, and Theatre Research International*.]

This attack on language led to such plays being labelled 'theatre of non-communication', which Ionesco objected to, claiming that he believed that people communicate only too well. What he wished to suggest was that the rational, discursive use of language was not the only, nor even the most powerful means by which people communicate. *Rhinocéros* contains a passage in which Jean, who is admonishing Bérenger for his moral laxity, and the Professor, who is conducting a logical argument on another part of the stage, end up saying exactly the same lines, echoing one another in perfect unison although their intended meanings are entirely different. The effect of this device is to arouse laughter in the audience and to discredit both rational discourse and the uses to which it is frequently put. The inarticulate roars of the rhinoceroses, however, are able to communicate directly with those who are beginning to feel tempted to join them. As they listen to the roarings and trumpetings, they are drawn like metal to a magnet straight out into the street to join the herd. In *La Leçon*, the Professor is able to rape and kill his pupil by means of the simple word *couteau* and in Jacques an ecstasy of orgasmic dimensions is achieved by the chanting of the word *chat*.

Rather than proclaiming non-communication, Ionesco displaces our attention from rational uses of language, refusing to treat it as central focus of the dramatic action. Instead of responding intellectually to his plays, Ionesco wants us, first and foremost, to respond with our senses. We witness a dramatic action in which things occur that are by turns shocking, funny, cruel, absurd. Illogicalities are left unexplained, paradoxes unresolved, but as the action progresses the tensions that are set up by this process generate a dramatic image of a nightmare world. (pp. 746)

In some ways Ionesco can in fact be best understood as a Surrealist dramatist. He has explained that his work originates, not from ideas, but from two basic states of consciousness, one of evanescence, light, release, the other of weight, opacity, confinement. His plays can all be interpreted as a struggle between these two forces, now one, now the other predominating. The paradoxical image of Amédée, at the end of *Amédée ou comment s'en débarrasser*, floating up into the sky suspended from the body that has formerly oppressed and crushed him is entirely Surrealist....

Ionesco himself has declared that, although interested as a young man in Surrealism, he is not a Surrealist. He accuses the Surrealists of having become fixated on manifestos and systems and he feels that he differs from them in his working methods.... But even if his methods do not always coincide, his fundamental aim, to liberate the subconscious levels of the mind from the straitjacket of logic and to achieve this by means of a dream-like style of theatre, is very similar to the programme of the early Surrealists. Although he rejects the name of Surrealist, Ionesco is a member of the Collège de Pataphysique, a mock-scholarly gathering devoted to the science of 'pataphysics' invented by Alfred Jarry, who defined it as 'the science of imaginary solutions'.

In the place of rational argument or neatly constructed plot, Ionesco relies upon dreams. He claims to have been strongly influenced by the Jungian concept that every man suffers from the separation between earth and sky. Only in childhood, during a holiday visit with his mother to the village of La Chapelle Athenaise, did he ever experience unity and harmony. This experience was like being taken right out of himself and finding the world around him totally transformed. For its short duration he experienced a feeling of indescribable bliss and total release so that even gravity seemed to lose its power over him. In many of his works he draws on memories of this experience of bliss and also of the moment when it left him. (p. 77)

In order to maintain the 'sharp' and 'pitiless' quality ('acuïté impitoyable') of [his] dreamed realities, Ionesco chooses to avoid conventional dramaturgical methods.... He repeatedly describes his plays as 'abstract theatre', 'pure dramas', in which the rise and fall of dramatic intensity should be compared more to that experienced when listening to music than to a conventional play. (p. 78) ( ... )

Ionesco's claim to have renewed language, conception and vision must depend for its justification upon his exploitation of the rich resources of the stage. Every element in his plays becomes a bearer of meaning. Inanimate objects are as important as animate ones. Since they conjure up a dream reality, the plays depend a lot on atmosphere, which is generated by the use of settings, lights, colours, sounds, and on unexpected transformations, as one character dissolves into another, or some basic law of nature is denied, as when Bérenger finds he can fly (in *Le Piéton de l'air*). For their thematic content the plays are much less original, dealing with the themes that have traditionally preoccupied European dramatists, such as freedom, guilt, love, death. The most important of these themes and the one that recurs most frequently is that of death, a subject that has always obsessed Ionesco.... *Le Roi se meurt* provides the most sustained example of a play on the theme of death in Ionesco's theatre. The dramatic rhythm of this long play is provided solely by King Bérenger's attempt to fight off the inevitable approach of death. The conflict in the play arises from his repeated attempts to restore his regal dignity which is repeatedly undercut by Marguerite and the Doctor. In King Bérenger is summed up the most consistent tragicomic tension in Ionesco's work: the attempts of men to assert their dignity in situations where they are merely laughable. He never appears to be more than a grotesque mockery of a king.... He stands as a figure for Everyman and the play follows a similar pattern to the medieval morality play of *Everyman*. As in that play, Bérenger finds himself gradually stripped of all things that he relied on for support: his wealth, his power, even his love for the young Queen Marie and, ultimately, his sense of selfhood. But unlike the medieval play, it does not end on a note of certainty. Rather than the soul ascending to be with Christ, we see nothing but a greyish light invading everything as Bérenger finally dies, the walls of his palace disappear and we are left with an immense, blank question mark.

> —David Bradby, "The Parisian Theatre II: The New Theatre." *Modern French Drama: 1940-1980*. Cambridge: University of Cambridge Press, 1984. 53-86.

## MATEI CALINESCU ON THE HISTORY BEHIND THE PLAY

[Matei Calinescu is a professor of Comparative Literature and West European Studies at Indiana University. He is the author of *Five Faces of Modernity* and *Rereading*. Calinescu's publications can also be found in *Poetics Today, Salmagundi, and Comparist*.]

Eugène Ionesco's conscious and unconscious memories of the Romanian 1930s and early 1940s accompanied him throughout his life and directly inspired one of his major plays, *Rhinoceros*, written in 1958. The rise in Romania of the extreme right-wing Iron Guard or Legionary movement and Ionesco's distressing experience of growing fanaticism among Romanian intellectuals, and even among his closest literary friends, was acknowledged by him as one of the sources of the play. Two other sources, noted by Ionesco in the preface to the first edition of the play (1961), sought to make the play more understandable to a western audience whose awareness of even the existence of Romania could not be taken for granted: a historical one reflected in the entry for 11 March 1936 in the published diary of Denis de Rougemont, who had witnessed in horror—"une horreur sacrée" as he specifies—a huge Nazi mass rally greeting its Fuhrer in a state of religious frenzy; and a literary one—Kafka's famous story "The Metamorphosis," in which the main character, Gregor Samsa, wakes up one morning inexplicably changed into a gigantic insect. In the preface, Ionesco refers directly to Denis de Rougemont's journal:

... Denis de Rougemont was staying in Germany, at Nuremberg, during a Nazi demonstration. He tells us how he found himself in the midst of a dense crowd awaiting the arrival of Hitler. The people were beginning to show signs of impatience when the Fuhrer and his entourage came in sight.... As they drew nearer ... the crowd gradually caught up in a kind of hysteria, frenziedly acclaiming the sinister man. The hysteria spread, and advanced, with Hitler, like a tide.... Denis de Rougemont tells us how uneasy he felt, how terribly alone in the crowd, offering hesitant resistance. His hair stood on end, literally he says, and then he understood what is meant by Holy Terror. Just then it was not his mind that resisted, not arguments formulated in his brain, but his whole being....

The reference to Denis de Rougemont helps Ionesco's reader/spectator to focus at once on the anti-Nazi character of the play and on the eventual feeling of radical aloneness of its main character, Bérenger. Reflecting on Kafka, whose name is often cited in Ionesco criticism, the reader/spectator may better grasp the playwright's use of the device of metamorphosis along lines that are, however, essentially different from Kafka's. One may note that Kafka's text, while teasing the reader's symbolic imagination, ultimately rejects interpretation in favor of an enigmatic literalness, whereas Ionesco's play is more conventionally allegorical, be it in an unconventionally farcical mode.

Considering the autobiographical Romanian inspiration of *Rhinoceros* will illuminate certain structural and psychological aspects of the play that neither de Rougemont nor Kafka can clarify: for instance, the sense of a progressive contagion by an initially rare and strange disease reaching epidemic proportions, a sense conveyed by the increasingly rapid rhythm in which people in the play's world change into rhinoceroses; and Bérenger's experience of witnessing in horror the metamorphosis of his closest friend (Jean), of his colleagues, and of his flame (Daisy), an experience not devoid of ambiguities, for it also brings about Bérenger's temptation to follow the others, to do as they do in order to avoid remaining alone.

A brief explanation of my method and purposes is in order here. The use of such terms as "sources" (textual, autobiographical) does not mean I am in favor of either "genetic" or "biographical" criticism, or, for that matter, in favor of any other sort of criticism, for here I speak not as a literary critic but as a cultural historian who tries to understand a literary work by whatever means—old or new—because that work itself might help to understand broader, metatextual trends and phenomena. More specifically, I am looking at *Rhinoceros* and its Romanian background in the hope of clarifying certain issues of national-cultural identity, cultural and political nationalism, voluntary ideological regimentation and its unexpected attractions for intellectuals, for young intellectuals especially, in the context of the Romanian 1930s and early 1940s, but also more generally. Ultimately, I am concerned less with *Rhinoceros* as a literary work and more with *Rhinoceros* as a model of understanding a specific historical situation with significant parallels in other European countries: the fascination of a generation of sophisticated intellectuals (in Romania the exceptions were few and the only major one was Ionesco himself) with the puerile, nebulous, primitive mysticism of the Iron Guard and its nearly inarticulate leader, Corneliu Codreanu. How could a bright young intelligentsia cave in to the dubious appeals of a sub-intellectual political movement, many of whose rank-and-fille militants were fanatic thugs? How could highly intelligent young people subscribe to the preposterous rituals and requirements of Legionary discipline? *Rhinoceros* does not give answers to such questions; but in illustrating, both comically and nightmarishly, the phenomenon of ideological contagion and the surrender of human individuality and intelligence to herdlike conformity, it brings us closer to understanding if not to explanation. And perhaps *Rhinoceros* can say something to us about the broader question of ideology and the responsibility of the intellectuals for spreading extreme ideologies (or, less frequently, resisting them).

The play *Rhinoceros* was derived from a short story with the same title, published in 1957 and describing, in the voice of an anonymous first-person narrator, the metamorphosis of people into rhinoceroses. The scene is an unnamed French provincial town on a Sunday: "We were sitting outside the cafe," the narrator starts his story, "my friend Jean and I, peacefully talking about one thing and another, when we caught sight of it on the opposite pavement, huge and powerful, panting noisily, charging straight ahead and brushing against market stalls—a rhinoceros." Jean is more surprised than the narrator who has a hangover after the previous Saturday night's alcoholic excesses; Jean is also more incensed by the notion that a rhinoceros is at large in town ("It ought not to be allowed," he exclaims preposterously). The following Sunday, under similar circumstances, a second rhinoceros rushes by the cafe and a discussion about it between the narrator and Jean (did it have one horn or two? was it an African or an Asian rhinoceros?) turns into a quarrel—Jean was overly touchy and "the slightest objection made him foam at the mouth" (80). The next day, a Monday, the narrator goes to work and learns that the chief clerk and other colleagues (Emile Dudard and the attractive secretary Daisy) had also spotted a stray rhinoceros. Only the freethinking Botard had not seen anything and refuses to believe in the "myth" of the rhinoceros: "Collective psychosis," he exclaims, quoting Marx without naming him, "just like religion, the opium of the people" (83). Soon after the entrance of Madame Boeuf, who has come to excuse her husband, the outside wooden stair to the office is pulled down by a two-horned rhinoceros, "trumpeting in an agonized and agonizing voice" (85); Madame Bouef recognizes her husband in the pachyderm and faints, while the rhinoceros goes on trumpeting tenderly. Once the Fire Brigade has rescued the stranded clerks, the narrator decides to pay a visit to Jean and apologize for having angered him the previous day. Jean is not feeling very well—it turns out that he has just started becoming a rhinoceros; naturally, his earlier opposition has been replaced by approving rationalizations. The following discussion takes place:

The narrator: "Do you know what happened to Boeuf? He's turned into a rhinoceros."

"Well, what about it? That's not such a bad thing! After all, rhinoceroses are creatures like ourselves, with just as much right to live ..."

"All the same, we have our own moral code, which I consider incompatible with that of these animals..."

"Humanism is out of date! You're a ridiculous old sentimentalist. You're talking nonsense."

Blind fury had disfigured his face.... The lump on his forehead had grown longer; he was staring fixedly at me, apparently without seeing me. Or, he must have seen me quite clearly, for he charged with his head lowered. I barely had time to leap to one side ... (89–90)

A little after Jean's metamorphosis, the narrator learns from Daisy that the chief clerk had also turned into a rhinoceros, followed by none other than the incredulous Botard, whose last words had been: "One must keep up with one's times." In the last scene of the story, the narrator, deeply in love with Daisy who has moved to his place, dreams out loud about having children with her and thus "regenerating humanity" like a new Adam and a new Eve—but she refuses. She promises, however, to stand fast with him "to the end" (96); but soon thereafter, one morning, the narrator finds her place in the bed empty. Alone and desperate, he feels that he will never be able to become a rhinoceros, like all the others, although he would like to.

> One day, looking at myself in a glass, I took a dislike to my long face: I needed a horn, or even two, to give dignity to my flabby features. (97)

And:

> Each morning I looked at my hands hoping that the palms would have hardened during my sleep. The skin remained flabby. I gazed at my too-white body, my hairy legs: oh for a hard skin and that magnificent green color, a decent, hairless nudity, like theirs! My conscience was increasingly uneasy, unhappy. I felt I was a monster.... I dared no longer look at myself. I was ashamed. And yet I couldn't, no, I couldn't. (97–8)

The play, which is of course longer and includes many specifically theatrical effects and developments, remains a remarkably faithful dramatization of the story, scene by scene, with no changes in the basic plot. There are, however, significant differences. The play makes more explicit (allegorically, politically) a dimension only implied in the more condensed and somewhat more dreamlike narrative version, by introducing the theme of "rhinoceritis," that is, by establishing a link between the Kafkaesque metamorphosis of people into beasts and the idea of disease, with its rich metaphorical potential. The disease, as already suggested, is a psychological epidemic, a collective "mental mutation" or a case of "mass hysteria." Its nature is ideological but the (extremist) ideology in question is not only undefined but also, paradoxically, mute: people are seduced into becoming rhinoceroses not by words, not by any sort of propaganda or argument, but by the sense of power that the rhinoceroses embody. All ideologies, Ionesco seems to imply, attract not by the programs they explicitly offer but by the implicit promise of access to power they make. It is in the name of such a promise of power that people voluntarily regiment themselves, that they give up their individuality and adopt an imitative, herdlike behavior, that they become fanatics. In his comments meant to clarify the meaning of the play, Ionesco has also insisted on the idolatrous and sectarian character of modern extremist ideologies:

> I wonder if I haven't hit on upon a new plague of modern times, a strange disease that thrives in different forms but is in principle the same. Automatic systematized thinking, the idol-ization of ideologies, screens the mind from reality, perverts our understanding and makes us blind. Ideologies ... get in the way of what we call co-existence, for a rhinoceros can only come to terms with one of his own kind, a sectarian with a member of his particular sect. (207)

Allegorically the play attempts to capture the inner logic of the two antithetical, if often strangely similar, totalitarian ideologies of our century, fascism and nazism on the one hand, and Stalinism in the broadest sense (including all communist-like kinds of intellectual behavior), on the other. Biographically, though, Ionesco's own experience of fascism, in the form of the Legionary movement, was both more intense and more directly threatening to him and to the values in which he believed than communism. He was fortunate enough not to live under communism in the country of his birth. However pervasive and obnoxious French communism and the forms of "political correctness" it generated might have been in the postwar years, Stalinism in Paris, embraced by many progressive intellectuals, bore no comparison with Stalinism in Moscow or in the capitals of the Soviet satellites. Communism in France, or the more anarchic and eclectic version of leftism that inspired the rebellious students of May 1968, while dominating intellectual life until the mid-1970s—even introducing a certain climate of unofficial leftist "censorship" and offering examples of opportunistic self-persuasion or "rhinocerization" never attained power, and its opponents, labeled "reactionary," "bourgeois," or whatever, could still express themselves and even become famous, as Ionesco's own case demonstrates. By the way, the accusations leveled at Ionesco by the Parisian Left that in the 1960s he had become a "right winger" are perfectly absurd: a philosophical anarchist and a staunch antinationalist and antifascist in Romania in the 1930s, someone who took an unpopular ethical stance, he remained the same nonconformist in postwar France, which meant opposing, from an embattled liberal-democratic position, the onslaught of leftist orthodoxy that was sweeping intellectual life; interestingly, when the French cultural climate changed in the late 1970s, some of his former leftist critics paid tribute to him not only as a writer but also as a generous supporter of dissidents from the Soviet Union and Eastern Europe as well as political refugees from various other dictatorships around the world. A closer familiarity with communism in power—as distinct from the ideological power of attraction of communism in Western Europe after the Second World War—might have prompted Ionesco to write a sequel to *Rhinoceros*, showing "rhinoceritis" in its more advanced stages: rhinoceroses even fiercer (but also secretly scared) after having lost their false convictions but not their hold on power; rhinoceroses clinging to their false convictions while becoming at the same time perfectly cynical; rhinoceroses pretending to be human; and more recently, some rhinoceroses undergoing a process of rehumanization.

*Rhinoceros*, Ionesco's major international success, owed its widespread appeal, apart from its dramatic qualities, its comic language, its rhythm, its original combination of wild farce and anxiety-ridden nightmare, to the ability of its central metaphor to designate suggestively, memorably, and succinctly a range of political-moral phenomena such as ideological radicalism, totalitarianism, fanaticism, imitation, herdlike behavior, extremism, collective self-persuasion, self-hypnosis, "political correctness," and so forth. In its own way, the funny and sinister notion of "rhinocerization" recalls other labels derived from literary works or, more often, from names of literary characters or authors: we speak of "Quixotic" natures and of "Quixotism"; we speak, in certain geographical and historical contexts, of "Bovarysme" (the French essayist Jules de Gaultier, who coined the term, wrote a whole book on it, *La philosophie du Bovarysme*, in 1912); closer to us in time and in experience, we speak of Kafkaesque bureaucracies or even circumstances (*Rhinoceros* itself presents a situation with definite Kafkaesque elements). All these are of course informal models of understanding, belonging to what we may call an informal epistemology, but one should not dismiss them for this reason. The insights to be gained through them cannot be gained by other means.

—Matei Calinescu, "Ionesco and *Rhinoceros:* Personal and Political Backgrounds." *East European Politics and Societies* 9, 3 (Fall 1995): 393-403.

## ROSETTE C. LAMONT ON BÉRENGER AS ANTIHERO

[Rosette C. Lamont is professor of French and Comparative literature, Graduate School and Queens College, City University of New York. Her publications include essays in *Massachusetts Review, Modern Drama, Grand Street, and Nottingham French Studies.* She has also published a book on Ionesco called *Ionesco's Imperatives*]

In *Rhinoceros* Ionesco demystifies the cult of rationalism, Descartes's legacy to Western culture. He shows that this philosophy can serve as blinders at a time of murderous violence. In the scene between Dudard and Bérenger, the latter may appear as hypochondriacal, even cowardly, but his anguish is a positive reaction to the germ of rhinoceritis. This angst is a symptom, like fever, suggestive of the fact that the sick body's struggle must begin before recuperation can occur. On the contrary, Dudard's superior attitude covers a wavering, ailing conscience.

True heroism for Ionesco is a quality of the heart rather than of the mind. It is the reaction of a modest man who wishes to remain true to himself. While the intellectual wavers, weighing abstract good against abstract evil, and letting real evil overtake him, the intuitive man rejects intuitively what he senses as destructive. Some intellectuals, such as Vaclav Havel, have been able to combine the qualities of the spirit with those of the mind. Despite polar conditions of life, neither Havel nor Ionesco have ever deviated from their path.

The final pages of *Rhinoceros* allow the reader and the audience to follow the tracing of this path. The penultimate scene is that between Bérenger and Daisy. The pretty secretary enters her colleague's room, a basket on her arm. She has brought him lunch. However, this innocent has witnessed a general panic in the office and the streets. M. Papillon (Mr. Butterfly), the head of the department, has joined the herd. Names from one of Ionesco's time capsules are added to that of the flitting creature: Cardinal de Retz, Mazarin, Saint-Simon. "All our great names!" exclaims Bérenger, who seems to have forgotten that they are those of political plotters, dishonest ministers, and literary gossips.

Bérenger and Daisy will also be caught in a time capsule. We are invited to travel through a telescoped future. The couple's conversation goes from a declaration of love to planning a family. However, the presence of rhino heads all around them is oppressive. Ionesco and his bride, Rodica Burileanu, must have felt much the same way in July, 1936, when they were married. Unlike Rodica, however, Daisy is not a true companion in days of misfortune. She wonders whether the rhinoceros world might not be in the right. As her fiancé speaks of their love, she exclaims: "I feel a bit ashamed of what you call love—this morbid feeling, this male weakness. And female too. It just doesn't compare with the ardour and tremendous energy emanating from all these creatures around us." Incensed, Bérenger slaps her face. They have come to the parting of ways. As Daisy says: "In a space of a few minutes we've gone through twenty-five years of married life." The life of the couple has been poisoned by the surrounding climate of opinion. As Daisy makes her escape to join the beastly mob, Bérenger remains alone, defiant yet terrified. He is the last human left on the face of this planet.

What makes Ionesco's protagonist fully human is the fact that he is racked by self-doubt. There is a moment in his soliloquy when he experiences a profound revulsion in regard to his weak body, pallid skin, hairy limbs, smooth brow. He cries out: "Oh, I'd love to have a hard skin in that wonderful dull green colour." The latter is a reminder of the Nazi uniforms.

No one who has seen the Nazi armored vehicles forging forward overrunning the nations they were determined to subjugate, will ever forget it. They seemed undefeatable, a Master Race, Wagnerian demigods. Their propaganda machine rolled in with their tanks, telling the conquered nations that they were weak, corrupt, sinful, and had brought this misfortune upon themselves. Many, like Bérenger, felt a kind of servile admiration for the discipline of people intent only on maintaining their well-oiled war machine. In the death camps, they took superhuman strides, in their greenish uniforms, shiny black boots, always accompanied by sleek attack dogs. The lice-covered, shivering prisoners were faced at every moment with the image of their inferior condition. Yet, those who came to doubt their right to exist were done for; they would not survive the camps.

Nor was there a way of communicating with these automatons. They shouted orders in a language many did not know, and if these orders were not instantly obeyed their whips spoke eloquently. Listening to their "Heils!" and military music, Bérenger wonders whether their raucous song may not have charm. He even tries to bellow as they do, but realizes he is incapable of learning their tongue. But what is the protagonist's language? What is he saying since he is the last creature to utter these sounds? He even wonders whether he understands what he is saying.

It is in this reflection that we may find a key to Ionesco's problematics of style and expression. Following this experience, it was no longer possible for Ionesco to entertain easy relations with the common tongue. As Elie Wiesel said at one of his public lectures: "Words in camp did not mean what they mean outside: 'hunger,' 'thirst,' 'bread.'" When Ionesco denies being an avant-garde writer, it is his way of saying that he does not experiment for the sake of experimentation. However, he is unable to take language for granted. The returning deportee, or exile, sees the once familiar world with the eyes of a stranger. Only then, when we come back among the living having visited the kingdom of the dying and the dead, do we have a chance to exist again.

The last man is much like the first. Alone among rhinoceroses, Bérenger is as grotesque as Adam among the animals of the newly fashioned planet. "I'm a monster, just a monster!" he shouts. Yet, there is no going back. The protagonist states defiantly:

> I'll take on the whole of them! I'll put up a fight against the lot of them, the whole lot of them! I'm the last man left, and I'm staying that way until the end. I'm not capitulating!

These last words have a Churchillian ring.

Bérenger, the shy dreamer given to fits of exaltation and spasms of anger, a fearful and yet audacious man, ineffectual at work, ill-adapted to society, often dependent on the small comfort of drink, flabby, paunchy, pallid, essentially kind and well-meaning, turns out to be our only champion. Unlikely as it seems—Ionesco wishes us to be aware of the paradox—when this man opposes evil, his act of defiance constitutes the triumph of each and every one of us. We are able to identify with this "man for our time," who has kept his decency among the mob of monsters. He is the emblem of our troubled epoch, an antihero who is a true hero, because he must.

—Rosette C. Lamont, "Bérenger: Birth of An Antihero." *Ionesco's Imperatives: The Politics of Culture.* Ann Arbor, Michigan: The University of Michigan Press, 1993. 145-148.

# Eugène Ionesco

*Elegii pentru fiintele mici*, 1934

*Nu*, 1934

*La cantatrice chauve*, 1950 – *The Bald Soprano* – *Kalju laulajatar*

*La lecon*, 1951 – *The Lesson* – *Oppitunti*

*Le salon de l'automobile*, 1953 – *The Motor Show*

*Amédée*, 1954 – trans.

*Les chaises*, 1954 – *The Chairs* – *Tuolit*

*Victimes du devoi*, 1954 – *Victims of Duty*

*Jacques, ou la soumission*, 1954 – *Jack, or the Submission*

*Le nouveau locataire*, 1955 – *The New Tenant* – *Uusi vuokralainen*

*Teur sans gages*, 1958 – *The Killer*

*L'impromptu de l'alma*, 1958 – *Improvisation*

*Le maitre*, 1958 – *The Leader*

*L'avenir est dans les (eufs*, 1958 – *The Future Is in the Egg)*

*Les rhoniceros*, 1959 – *Rhinoceros* – *Sarvikuonot*

*La vase*, 1961

*Notes et contra-notes*, 1962

*La photo du colonel*, 1962 – *The Colonel's Photograph*

*Le roi se meurte*, 1962 – *Exit the King* – *Kuningas kuolee*

*Notes et contre notes*, 1962 – *Notes and Counter Notes*

*Le pieton de l'air*, 1963 – *A Stroll in the Air* – *Jalankulkija ilmassa*

*Delire à deux*, 1963 – *Frenzy for Two or More*

*Le tableau*, 1963 – *The Picture*

*La colere*, 1963 – *Anger*

*Scene a quartre*, 1963 – *Foursome*

*La soif et la faim*, 1964 – *Hunger and Thirst*

*Notes and Counter Notes: Writing on Theatre*, 1964

*La lacune*, 1966 – *The Gap*

*Au pied du mur,* 1966

*Entreties avec claude bonnefoy,* 1966

*Lecons de Francais pour americains,* 1966

*La soif et la faim,* 1966 – *Hunger and Thirst*

*Journal en miettes,* 1967 – *Fragments of a Journal*

*The Colonel's Photograph,* 1967

*Present passe passe present,* 1968 – *Present Past Past Present*

*Fragments of a Journal,*1968

*Jeux de massacre,* 1970 – *Killing Game*

*Decouverst,* 1970

*Discours de reception d'Eugène Ionesco à L'academie Francaise et
    reponse de Jean Delay,* 1971

*Macbett,* 1972 – *Macbeth*

*Ce formidable bordel,* 1973 – *A Hell of a Mess / What a Bloody Circus!*

*Le solitaire,* 1973 – *The Hermit – Erakko*

*L'homme aux valises,* 1975 – *Man with Bags*

*Antidotes,* 1977

*Why Do I Write?: A Summing Up,* 1978

*Un homme en question,* 1979

*Theme et varations; ou, voyages chex les morts,* 1980 – *Journey
    among the Dead*

*Voyages chez les morts,* 1981

*Le blank et le noir,* 1981

*Hugoliades,* 1982

*Theatre,* 1954-1981 *(7 vols.)*

*Razboi cu toata lumea [War with the whole world],*1992

# Eugène Ionesco

Barsam, Joyce Shushan. "Individuation or the Search for Self in the Theater of Ionesco," Diss. Tufts University, 1989.

Blume, Marie. "A Work Is Not a Series of Answers It Is a Series of Questions ... It Is Not the Answer that Enlightens, but the Question", *International Herald Tribune*, (Jan. 1970) 10-11.

Bonnefoy, Claude. "Conversations with Eugène Ionesco." Translated by Jan Dawson. London: Faber and Faber, 1970; New York, Holt, Rinehart and Winston, 1971.

Bradley, E. I. "The Search for Individual Identity in the Works of Ionesco, 1950-1985," Diss. Durham, 1986.

Bree, Germaine et Alexander Kroff. "Ionesco." *Twentieth Century French Drama*, London, Macmillan, 1969.

Cismaru, Alfred. "Ionesco the Rhinoceros" *Texas Quarterly*, vol. 6, 2, (1966).

Coe, Richard N. "The Meaning of Un-Meaning" *Aspects of Drama and the Theatre*, Sydney U.P., 1965.

———. "Ionesco." New York: Barnes and Noble, Inc., 1965.

———. "Eugène Ionesco – a study of his work," Evergreen Black Cat book B-235 (USA), 1970.

———. "Ionesco: a study of his plays" (Contains a translation by Richard N. Coe of an early and hitherto unpublished Ionesco text, "The Niece-Wife"), London: Methuen, 1971.

———. "On Being Very, Very Surprised: Ionesco and the Vision of Childhood," *The Dream and the Play: Ionesco's Theatrical Quest* ed. Moshe Lazar, New York, 1978.

Cohn, Ruby. "Bérenger, protagonist of an anti-playwright." *Modern Drama*, vol. VIII, 1965.

———. "Four Stages of Absurdist Hero" *Drama Survey*, hiver 1965.

Coleman, Ingrid H. "The Professor's Dilemma: The Absurd Comic Principle in Ionesco's La Leçon," *Perspectives on Contemporary Literature*, tome 7, 1981: 44-53.

Coleman, Ingrid H. "Memory into 'Message': The Forgetting of the Myth of Origins in Ionesco's Les Chaises," *Perspectives on Contemporary Literature*, tome 9, 1983: 60-68.

Coleman Chafee, Ingrid "The Comic and the Sacred: The Rite of Passage in Ionesco's Le Roi se Meurt," *Journal of the Association for the Interdisciplinary Study of the Arts*, vol. 2, Fall 1996: 77-86.

Coleman Chafee, Ingrid "Conquering Gravity: Flight and the Joy of Creation in the Plays of Eugène Ionesco," *Journal for the Association of the Interdisciplinary Study of the Arts*, vol. 5, No. 1, Fall 1999: 83-92.

Corrigan, Robert W. "The Theater of Ionesco: The Ghost and Primal Dialogue." *The dream and the play. Ionesco's theatrical quest* Moshe Lazar ed. Malibu, California, undena Publ., VIII, 1982.

Craddock, George Edward Jr. "The Concept of Identity in the Theatre of Eugène Ionesco," Ph.D. thesis (unpublished), Louisiana State University, 1966.

Craddock, George Edward Jr. "Escape and Fulfillment in the Theatre of Ionesco," *Southern Quarterly* 10, Oct. 1971: 15-22.

Driver, Tom F. "Ionesco's Place in Contemporary Theatre" T.D.: *Romantic Quest and Modern Query*, Delacorte Press, New York, 1970: 346-390.

Eastman, Richard M. "Experiment and Vision in Ionesco's Plays," *Modern Drama* vol. IV, 1961-62: 3-19.

Edney, David. "The Family and Society in the Plays of Ionesco," *Modern Drama* vol. 28, 3, 1985: 377-399.

Ellis, Mary H. "The Work of Eugène Ionesco," Southern *Quarterly* vol. 2, April 1964: 220-235.

Esslin, Martin. "Ionesco and the Creative Dilemma," *The Tulane Drama Review* 7: 3, New Orleans, 1963: 169-179.

Friedman (Eds.). *The Two Faces of Ionesco* (pp. 5-19). Troy, NY: The Whitston Publishing Company.

Gaensbauer, Deborah B. "Dreams, myths and politics in Ionesco's *L'Homme aux Valises*," *Modern Drama* XXVIII, 1985: 388-396.

———. "Eugène Ionesco Revisited" (Twayne's World Author Series, 863), Nov. 1996.

Gerrard, Charlette F. "Bergsonian elements in Ionesco's *Le Piéton de l'Air*," *Papers on Language and Literature* 9, 1973: 297-310.

———. "Pestilence in contemporary French drama." *Symposium* 31, 1977: 302-322.

Ghitulescu, Emil "Final act" *Romanian Panorama*, Bucuresti, nr. 5-6, 1994.

Glicksberg, Charles. "Ionesco and the Aesthetics of the Absurd," Arizona *Quarterly* vol. 18, 1962: 293-303.

———. "Ionesco and the Comedy of the Absurd." *The Literature of Nihilism*, Bucknell University Press, 1975: 222-233.

Griffith, Hughes & Ruth Bury. "Eugène Ionesco. A Bibliography" (1310 titles). Cardiff, University of Wales Press, 1974.

Guicharnaud, Jacques & June. "The Weight of Things: Ionesco," *Modern French Theatre*, New Haven, London, 1967: 215-229.

Guthke, Karl Siegfried. "The Modernity of Tragicomedy," *K.S.G. Modern Tragicomedy: An Investigation into the Nature of the genre*. New York, Random House, 1966: 95-134.

Hayman, R. *Contemporary Playwrights: Eugène Ionesco*. London, Great Britain: Heinemann Educational Books. (1972).

Henry III, William A. "Fascism, Fury, Fear, and Farce: Eugène Ionesco's absurdist comedies transmuted a century of dictatorship and evil into profound nonsense and guffaws." *TIME Domestic*, vol. 143, 15.

Hesson, Ian Matthew. "The Worlds of Eugène Ionesco. His Political Views and His Dramatic Art" unpublished Ph.D. Thesis. Bedford College, Royal Holloway Library, University of London.

Hill, Linda. "The Language of Monsters: Ionesco's *Jacques au la Soumission*" *Language as Aggression. Studies in Postwar Drama*, Linda Hill, ed, Bonn, Bouvier, 1976: 14-37.

Homan, Sidney. "The Audience As Actor and Character: The Modern Theatre of Beckett, Brecht, Genet, Ionesco, Pinter, Stoppard, and Williams," 1989.

Jacobs, Gabriel. "Ionesco and the critics: E. Ionesco interviewed by G. Jacobs" *Critical Inquiry* 1, 3, March 1975: 641-654.

Jacobsen, J., & Mueller, W. R. *Ionesco and Genet*. New York: Hill and Wang, 1968.

Jacquart, Emmanuel. "Interview with Ionesco," *Diacritics* 3, p. 45-48, 1973.

Kern, Edith. "Ionesco and Shakespeare, *Macbeth* on the Modern Stage," *South Atlantic Bulletin*, 39, Jan. 1974: 3-16.

Kitchin, Lawrence. "Theater, nothing but theater: the plays of Eugène Ionesco" *Encounter*, 4, 1958.

Klaver, Elizabeth. "Postmodernism and Metatextual Space in the Plays of Beckett, Ionesco, Albee and Mamet," *Dissertation Abstracts International* 2377A, University of California, Riverside, 1990.

Kluback, William and Michael Finkenthal. "The Clown in the Agora: Conversations about Eugène Ionesco," 1998.

Knapp, Bettina L. "Introduction to 'Les Chaises,'" Jacques Guicharnaud, Paris Book Center Inc. New York, 1967. 595-644.

————. "Ionesco's Plays A Conspiracy of the Mind," *Twentieth-Century European Drama* (edited by Brian Docherty, Goldsmiths College, University of London), Oct. 1993.

Kyle, Linda Davis. "Ionesco: A Selective Bibliography, 1974-1978," *Bulletin of Bibliography* vol. 37, 1980: 167-184.

Lamont, Rosette C. "The Metaphysical Farce: Beckett and Ionesco," *French Review* 31, Feb. 1959.

————. "The Proliferation of matter in Ionesco's plays," *French Review*, 1962.

————. "The hero in spite of himself," *Yale French Studies* 29, New Haven, 1962: 73-81.

————. "Air and Matter," *French Review* vol. 38, 1965: 349-361.

————. "Entretien avec Ionesco," Cahiers *Renaud-Barrault* 53, Feb. 1966: 26-29.

————. "Ionesco: A Collection of Critical Essays." Englewood Cliffs, NJ: Prentice-Hall, Inc., 1967, 1973.

————. "An interview with Eugène Ionesco," *The Massachusetts Review* 10, 1, hiver 1969: 128-148.

————. "From Macbeth to Macbett," *Modern Drama* 15, Dec. 1972: 231-253.

————. "The Double Apprenticeship: Life and the process of dying," *The Phenomenon of Death* (ed. E. Wyschsogrod), Harper & Row, 1973.

————. "Ionesco's Imperatives – The Politics of Culture," *The first complete survey in English of Ionesco's contributions to the stage, and a new recognition of their political content.* University of Michigan Press, 1993.

Lamont, Rosette C. & Melvin J. Friedman, ed "The two Faces of Ionesco." The Whitston Publishing Company, Troy, New York, 1978.

Lane, Nancy (1947-). "Understanding Eugène Ionesco," University of South Carolina Press, 1994.

Lazar, Moshe, ed. "The Dream and the Play: Ionesco's Theatrical Quest" (contient les communications du Colloque Ionesco organisé à UCLA de Los Angeles (24-26 April 1980), Malibu, California, Undina Publications, 1982.

Lewis, Allan, *Ionesco.* New York: Twayne Publishers, 1972.

Mc Auley, Gay. "An Analysis of Dramatic Method in the Plays of Beckett and Ionesco," Ph.D. thesis (unpublished), University of Bristol, 1969.

Miller, Henry. "Try Ionesco," *Monterey Peninsula Herald,* (October 28, 1959), 36.

————. "The Music of Ionesco," *Monterey Peninsula Herald,* (November 4, 1959), 26.

————. "Ionesco's Soprano Punched a Time Clock," *Monterey Peninsula Herald,* (November 30, 1959), 20.

————. "Ionesco's Soprano Punched a Time Clock," *Between Worlds,* I (Summer 1960), 99-112.

Moore, Harry T. "The Antitheatre of Ionesco," *H.T.M.: Twentieth Century literature since World War II,* Heinemann, London, 1969: p. 154-161, .

Murray, J. "Ionesco and the mechanics of memory," *Yale French Studies* 29, 1962: 82-87.

Parker, R.B. "The theory and the theatre of the absurd" *Queen's Quarterly* 73, 1965.

Pronko, Leonard Cabell. "Eugène Ionesco," New York, Columbia University Press, (Columbia essays on modern writers, no. 7) 1965.

Purdy, S.B. "A reading of Ionesco's 'The Killer,'" *Modern Drama.* Feb. 1968. 416-423.

Reeves, Geoffrey et Tim Corrie. "Conversation with Ionesco," *New Magazine* 6, 3, 1965: 4-7.

Revel, J.-F. "The Young Ionesco," *Encounter* LXVIII, 2, Feb. 1987.

Rigg, Patricia. "Ionesco's Bérenger: Existential Philosopher or Philosophical Ironist?" *Modern Drama* 7, 1992.

Rosenberg, M. "A metaphor for dramatic form," *Journal of Aesthetics and Art Criticism*, 17, Baltimore, 1958/59: p. 174-180.

Roud, Richard. "The opposite of sameness," Encore, London, June-July 1957.

Rozik, Dr. Eli. "Stage Metaphor: With or Without – On Rina Yerushalmi's Production of The Chairs by Ionesco." *Theatre Research International*, 19: 2, 1994.

Schechner, R. "Three Aspects of Ionesco's Theater," Ph.D. thesis (unpublished), Tulane University, 1962.

———. "The enactment of the 'Not' in Ionesco's *Les Chaises*." *Yale French Studies* 29, 1962: 65-72.

———. "An Interview with Ionesco," *Tulane Drama Review* 7: 3, 1963: 163-168.

———. "The Inner and Outer Reality," *Tulane Drama Review* 7: 3, 1963: 187-217.

Selz, Jean. "The world of Ionesco." *International Theatre Annual* 2, Harold, Holson, London, 1957 + *Tulane Drama Review* III, 1.10., 1958.

Stack, R. "Ionesco's Art of Derision," *Plays and Players*, 7, June 1960.

Steel, David. "Ionesco and Rattigan ... or Watson at the Theatre Tonight?" *French Studies Bulletin*, 41 (1991-1992).

Strem, George C. "Ritual and Poetry in Eugène Ionesco's Theatre," *Texas Quarterly* vol. 5, 4, 1962: 149-158.

Strem, W.P.H. "The Anti-Theatre of E. Ionesco" *Twentieth Century Literature* 16, Melbourne, 1962: 70-83.

Thomson, Peter. "Games and Plays: An Approach to Ionesco" *Educational Theatre Journal* 22, I, March 1970: 60-70.

Vos, Nelvin. "Eugène Ionesco and Edward Albee; a critical essay. (Series: Contemporary writers in Christian perspective) Grand Rapids, Michigan, éd. William B. Eerdmans 1968.

# ACKNOWLEDGMENTS

*"The Bald Soprano, The Lessons, The Chairs"* by Allan Lewis from *Ionesco* © 1972 by Twayne Publishers, Inc. Reprinted by permission of the Gale Group.

*"The Bald Soprano* and *The Lesson*: An Inquiry into Play Structure" by Richard Schechner from *Ionesco: A Collection of Critical Essays"* © 1973 by Richard Schechner. Reprinted by permission.

"Condemned to Exist" by Alfred Schwarz from *Buchner to Beckett: Dramatic Theory and the modes of Tragic Drama* (Ohio University Press, 1978) © 1978 by Alfred Schwarz. Reprinted by permission.

"Bobby Watson and the Philosophy of Language" by Michael Issacharoff from *French Studies* XLVI, no. 3 © 1992 by The Society of French Studies. Reprinted by permission.

"Theater of the Absurd: *The Bald Soprano* and *The Lesson*" by Nancy Lane from *Understanding Eugène Ionesco* © 1994 by the University of South Carolina Press. Reprinted by permission.

"Ionesco's *The Bald Soprano*" by John V. McDermott from *Explicator* 55, no. 1. Reprinted by permission of the Helen Dwight Reid Educational Foundation. Published by Heldref Publications, 1319 Eighteenth St., NW, Washington, DC 20036-1802 © 1996.

*"The Bald Soprano* and *The Lesson:* An Inquiry into Play Structure" by Richard Schechner from *Ionesco: A Collection of Critical Essays* © 1973 by Prentice Hall. Reprinted by permission.

"Philology Can Lead to the Worst" by Michel Benamou from *The Two Faces of Ionesco*, Eds. Rosette C. Lamont and Melvin J. Friedman © 1978 by The Whitson Publishing Company. Reprinted by permission.

"Mythic Dimensions and Modern Classics" by Christopher Innes from *Holy Theatre: Ritual and the Avant Garde* © 1981 Christopher Innes. Reprinted by permission.

"The Logic of Ionesco's *The Lesson*" by Michael Wreen from *Philosophy and Literature* vol. 7, no. 2 © 1983 by *Philosophy and Literature*. Reprinted by permission.

---

INDEX OF

# Themes and Ideas